DAYTRIPS and
GETAWAY WEEKENDS

in Vermont, New Hampshire, and Maine

Help Us Keep This Guide Up-to-Date

Every effort has been made by the authors and editors to make this guide as accurate and useful as possible. However, many things can change after a guide is published—establishments close, phone numbers change, facilities come under new management, and so on.

We would love to hear from you concerning your experiences with this guide and how you feel it could be improved and kept up-to-date. While we may not be able to respond to all comments and suggestions, we'll take them to heart, and we'll also make certain to share them with the authors. Please send your comments and suggestions to the following address:

The Globe Pequot Press
Reader Response/Editorial Department
P.O. Box 480
Guilford, CT 06437

Or you may e-mail us at:

editorial@globe-pequot.com

Thanks for your input, and happy travels!

DAYTRIPS and GETAWAY WEEKENDS

in Vermont, New Hampshire, and Maine

by PATRICIA and ROBERT FOULKE

The Globe Pequot Press

Guilford, Connecticut

Cover photo by Jane Sapinsky/Stock Market
Maps by William L. Nelson Cartography & Graphics

ISSN: 1536-6219
ISBN: 0-7627-1063-2

Manufactured in the United States of America
First Edition/First Printing

The prices and rates listed in this guidebook were confirmed at press time. We recommend, however, that you call establishments to obtain current information before traveling.

Contents

Contents

Introduction

A northern New England daytrip, weekend, or vacation offers remarkable variety to the imaginative traveler. Whether you live around the corner or across the country, something new awaits you on each trip. You may enjoy an Atlantic sunrise or a Green Mountain sunset, undisturbed saltwater marshes or busy village greens, fresh lobster in Maine or local cheese in Vermont. You might hike the Appalachian Trail, run white water on the Allagash, and climb in the Presidential Range. Or you can explore maritime museums and reconstructed colonial villages, walk historic trails in old cities, trace local legends and the lore of shipwrecks, and collect valuable memories everywhere.

For forty-eight years we have enjoyed these many pleasures of New England. During this time we have traveled with babies and toddlers, children and teenagers, and alone. We have discovered the pleasures of traveling light and the problems of carrying too much in a backpack or the trunk of a car. At times we have tried to do too much, planning our trips in great detail; at others we have simply taken off on an impromptu journey with vague destinations. But no matter how we have traveled, and no matter how often we have visited a place, we have never exhausted the possibilities of this region blessed by mountain, sea, city, and a rich cultural heritage. If this book helps you to enjoy New England as much as we have, we will be content.

Trip Planning

This book suggests a variety of activities to suit travelers with different inclinations. For those with strong historical interests, we have interviewed people with great expertise on the staffs of the museums and old houses listed in each itinerary. Often these individuals have provided more information than we can use in a book of this size, but we have included enough of it to whet your appetite and give you some background for your visit to each site. For those who want to build a trip around doing more than seeing, we have indicated special recreational opportunities, such as

climbing the ravines of Mount Washington or canoeing in wild white water on the West River in Jamaica, Vermont.

Within a city or region, we have tried to cluster or group sites together so that you will know what is available nearby. We don't like to drive or walk back and forth randomly looking for something and know you won't want to either. For your convenience, we have also suggested a place or two for lunch or dinner in many areas. The Appendix also lists some interesting inns, historic hotels, resorts, and bed-and-breakfast homes so that you can call ahead to make a reservation if you wish; well-known motel chains are not included. These suggestions for meals and accommodations are not comprehensive for any area or evaluative, either by inclusion or omission. We are not involved in rating places to eat or stay, by price or by quality, but those listed are ones that we or our friends have enjoyed.

Itineraries

Styles of travel involve choices that ultimately reflect styles of personality. We opt for a flexible mode of travel midway between the carefully integrated schedule of a business trip and the total freedom of impulsive wandering. Our planned itineraries will save you the time and trouble of gathering information and deciding on a route in a new region, but they need not confine you. You can choose to travel all or part of any trip or combine parts of several. The itineraries are grouped by states, and you can connect easily from one itinerary to another within or between states. Maps show the route from place to place so that you can visualize the possible connections and permutations that are most appealing to you.

Each itinerary contains sightseeing tips and a good bit of detail about places of special interest. The description is not meant to be comprehensive, but it represents a selection of the highlights of each site or place, as well as some little-noticed details that may convey some sense of ambience. At times our enthusiasm runs away with us and we write a great deal; in those cases we hope you will enjoy sharing our bent for personal discovery. We also hope that our tracks will lead to new ones of your own making. We never intended "doing" New England and tying it up in a neat package to be unwrapped by docile readers. We know that there is much that we have missed, whole areas unopened to our imaginations, and much that we can revisit with benefit. The value of travel lies in the process, not the product.

The Green Mountains of Vermont and the Champlain Valley. Ethan Allen's beautiful ridge of mountains—the backbone of Vermont separating the rest of New England from the Champlain Valley—is prized today by skiers, hikers, and sightseers who want to admire contours of rounded beauty. To the west, Lake Champlain provides a major water link between the St. Lawrence and the Hudson that played a large part in determining the outcome of the French and Indian War and the American Revolution.

Southern Vermont. In the southern tier of Vermont, mountains and valley towns merge into an extraordinary landscape that pleases the eye at every curve of the road. There is more fine skiing and hiking here, as well as lots to see—covered bridges, country stores, picture-book villages surrounding greens, churches with layered steeples, cheese factories, bowl mills, potteries, and maple sugar huts.

The New Hampshire Shore. Settlers arrived here, after months at sea, to find wild strawberries growing along the banks of the Piscataqua River. Historic homes in Portsmouth and surrounding towns reflect the evolution of seacoast life through four centuries.

Southern New Hampshire and The Lake District. Formed by glaciers, the lakes of central New Hampshire are dotted with islands and carved with coves that make them perfect for summer holidays. Midway through the southern tier of the state, the broad valley of the Merrimack River gives way to the ridges and hills surrounding Mount Monadnock.

The White Mountains of New Hampshire. The highest mountains in New England provide a challenge for skiers and climbers, as well as an extensive network of huts and trails for hikers. Many of the mountains' wide vistas and unusual rock formations are also accessible by road, aerial tramway, and cog railway.

Down East along the Coast of Maine. Sailors ran downwind in prevailing southwesterlies as they moved northeastward along this coast, thereby creating the otherwise incomprehensible phrase "Down East." This rugged coastline of fjords created by long peninsulas with secure harbors and saltwater farms has always been more accessible by sea than by land, and its interpenetration of land and sea continues to attract artists, sailors, and travelers.

The Lakes and Mountains of Maine. The justly famous shore is not all there is to Maine. Its vast interior filled with large lakes, mountain ranges, and river networks provides the most extensive wilderness area in New England, stretching from the Longfellow Mountains, Baxter State Park, and the Allagash Wilderness Waterway to the Canadian border.

The Armchair Traveler

As we traveled doing the research for this book we became increasingly excited by the rare opportunity we have—to learn more about the rich historical heritage of these states and then to have the fun of writing about it for others. As children we had a smattering of historical background about this part of the country from books, but we had no sense of the blending of past and present that we now feel as we walk the streets of most New England towns. Whether you will be taking a trip or traveling vicariously from your armchair, we hope to intrigue you with historical tales of real people who lived long ago.

It's impossible to think about New England without considering the history of the area—a history embellished with centuries-old folktales and legends. Throughout the book we've scattered ghost stories, local tall tales, and anecdotes—all to whet your appetite for this marvelous region of our nation.

Visitor Information

We usually begin by attacking the Internet, which offers information galore. But remember that much of the Internet—unlike a published book—is unedited, and Web sites for places to eat and stay are just another form of advertising. State tourist offices offer maps, information about historic sites, and lists of campgrounds and other accommodations, restaurants, and sightseeing suggestions. It's a good idea to write or call before you go.

Vermont

Vermont Travel Division, 61 Elm Street, Montpelier, VT 05602; (800) 837–6668 or (802) 828–3236; fax: (802) 828–3233

New Hampshire

New Hampshire Office of Vacation Travel, 172 Pembroke Road, Concord, NH 03302; (800) 386–4664 or (603) 271–2343; fax: (603) 271–2629

Maine

Maine Tourism Association, Box 2300, Hallowell, ME 04347; (800) 782–6497 or (207) 623–0363
State of Maine Tourism Office, 109 Sewall Street, Augusta, ME 04333; (888) 624–6345; fax: (207) 287–8070

You can also write to individual chambers of commerce in the towns you intend to visit. They too offer maps and information about historic houses in the area, restaurants, accommodations, and special activities.

A number of organizations publish information about wildlife sanctuaries, wilderness expeditions, hiking trails, and outdoor recreation: The **Appalachian Mountain Club** (5 Joy Street, Boston, MA 02108; 617–523–0636) is the oldest conservation club in the United States. It publishes guidebooks on hiking trails and canoe routes, a monthly newsletter, and a semiannual journal. **The National Audubon Society** (950 Third Avenue, New York, NY 10022; 212–832–3200) maintains wildlife sanctuaries all over the country. Its programs include conservation education, research on current wildlife issues, and natural history films. The society also operates libraries and stores where you can buy nature-related gifts. **The Green Mountain Club** (Box 889, Montpelier, VT 05602; 802–244–7037) maintains and protects the Long Trail system and offers guidebooks and maps. **American Youth Hostels** (891 Amsterdam Avenue, New York, NY 10012; 212–932–2300) offers hiking and bicycle tours and a network of low-cost hostels.

Activities

Enjoy! Let the ages and interests of your family or group set the focus of your trip. But leave some time free for relaxation (defined as time to do nothing) and flexibility (the freedom to change your mind according to weather and mood).

When our children were young, we chose activities to appeal to their interests and levels of understanding. We visited zoos, country fairs, beaches, whaling museums, aquariums, restored villages, dinosaur traces, amusement parks, and planetariums; we took train rides and steamboat trips; we saw theater and puppet shows, baseball games, and historical reenactments; and we canoed and sailed and swam and rowed. Whenever we could we prepared them for an activity—showing them pictures and talking about the historic sites we intended to visit. They especially loved hearing stories about the children who once lived in the old houses we would tour.

We let them guide us through museums, picking out displays that intrigued them rather than stopping them (shifting from one foot to the other) in front of every exhibit. Then we would head for the museum shop and select postcards for our collections.

Children love nature trails with buttons to push and signs to read. They also love hikes, especially when they're well supplied with goodies for energy. Ours carried hard candies, raisins, fruit, gorp, and a jacket in a child-sized rucksack. And as we went along, we'd decorate the rucksack with souvenir patches from places we visited.

Whether you're traveling alone or with family, try something new on each trip. For starters, think about lake canoeing, whitewater rafting and kayaking, saltwater fishing, gliding, distance swimming, snorkeling, cross-country skiing, or something else that appeals to you.

Extend your travels! We invite you to explore southern New England's history, culture, and scenic landscapes in our companion book, *Daytrips and Getaway Weekends in Connecticut, Rhode Island, and Massachusetts.*

Vermont

The Green Mountain State

The early history of human habitation in Vermont begins with the Algonquins about 2000 B.C. Later the Iroquois, Mohicans, and Abenakis passed through Vermont trails to get from Massachusetts to New York. This Native American heritage is still very much present in the names around the state: Quechee, Bomoseen, Passumpsic, Winooski, Jamaica.

On July 4, 1609, Samuel de Champlain led Algonquin Indians in an encounter against the Iroquois. He killed two Iroquois chiefs and a number of warriors, incurring the wrath of the Iroquois for years to come. While here he named a mountain *Le Lion Couchant* (the resting lion); it's known today as Camel's Hump. And he called the largest island in Lake Champlain Grand Isle. This French influence is also evident in other regional names: Montpelier, Vergennes, St. Johnsbury, Danville, and of course, the state's name itself: *Vermont,* meaning "green mountains."

The first English settlement in the area was Fort Dummer, near Brattleboro, in 1724. The land was bought at auction by Sir William Dummer and Colonel William Brattle (Dummerston and Brattleboro were named for them). At that time Vermont was part of New York, which didn't keep New Hampshire's Governor Wentworth from annexing land and granting it to settlers. The matter was settled by King George II, who maintained that the land belonged to New York. In 1770 Ethan Allen and his Green Mountain Boys rallied to drive off the "Yorkers" who were following up on that claim.

This group also responded to the call against the British during the Revolution. Jointly led by Allen and Colonel Benedict Arnold, the Green Mountain Boys captured Fort Ticonderoga in a surprise raid on May 10, 1775. This raid early in the war was especially important in an unexpected way, giving Americans control of the fort's cannon, which Henry Knox then hauled across Massachusetts to help drive the British out of Boston. In 1777 Vermont declared itself an independent republic, which it remained for fourteen years before becoming a state.

The Green Mountains are probably the remains of the oldest mountain range in New England, dating back 440 million years. Erosion worked folds into the bedrock on a north-south axis, producing an even, rolling range with no jagged peaks or deep valleys. This peneplain, or flat plain, is interspersed with monadnocks, isolated mountains made up of very hard bedrock that did not erode as much as the land around it.

There are not many lakes in the Green Mountains, possibly because the movement of the glaciers was along the folds southward instead of across them. There was, however, one large glacial lake, Lake Vermont, which covered the Champlain lowland up to 700 feet above the present level of Lake Champlain.

Although the Green Mountains are fairly low and rounded in the south, farther north they divide into three parallel ranges more rugged in appearance and filled with more separate peaks. Mount Killington, Mount Ellen, Camel's Hump, and Mount Mansfield are all over 4,000 feet high. Some geologists believe that the mountains in the south were once much higher. They claim that the Taconic Mountains, which stretch between northern Connecticut and central Vermont on a north–south axis, were once the tops of the southern Green Mountains, which detached and moved a number of miles to the west. (This is called a thrust fault—an older rock formation settled over a younger one.)

Touring by car in Vermont brings special pleasures to those not in a hurry, including the simple pleasures of driving well-paved, curving roads through beautiful landscape. Each vista provides a new perspective on trees and mountains, and you will come upon immaculate villages built around central greens, church spires with individual character, elegantly simple colonial houses, and a host of other surprises. One of those surprises is likely to be a covered bridge, either on your route or adjacent to it. And there are more than a hundred to find. See a Vermont state map for their locations, or check www.vermontbridges.com. If you are keen on covered bridges you may also want to consult Ed Barna's *Covered Bridges of Vermont* (call the author at 802–247–3146 for an autographed copy) or Joseph Nelson's *Vermont's Covered Bridges*.

For More Information

Vermont's system of providing visitor information is quite centralized. The major sources are:

Vermont Chamber of Commerce, P.O. Box 37, Montpelier, VT 05601; (802) 223–3443; www.vtchamber.com

Vermont Department of Tourism and Marketing, 134 State Street, Montpelier, VT 05602; (802) 828–3237; www.travelvermont.com

In addition, there are five welcome centers, two on the Canadian border (on I–89, 802–868–3244 and on Route 2, Alburg, 802–254–4593), and one each on the Massachusetts border (on I–91, 802–254–4593), the New Hampshire border (on I–93, 802–748–9368), and the New York border (on Route 4A, 802–265–4763).

For more specialized information contact the following:

Vermont Attractions Association, Box 1284, Montpelier, VT 05601; (802) 229–4581; www.vtattractions.org

Vermont Department of Fish and Wildlife, 103 South Main Street, 10 South, Waterbury, VT 05671; (802) 241–3711; www.anr.state.vt.us/fw/fwhome

Vermont Department of Forests and Parks, 103 South Main Street, 10 South, Waterbury, VT 05671; (802) 241–3655; www.vtstateparks.com

Vermont Ski Areas Association, P.O. Box 368, Montpelier, VT 05601; (802) 223–2439; www.skivermont.com

Vermont Lodging and Restaurant Association, 3 Main Street, Ste. 106, Burlington, VT 05401; (802) 660–9001; www.visitvt.com

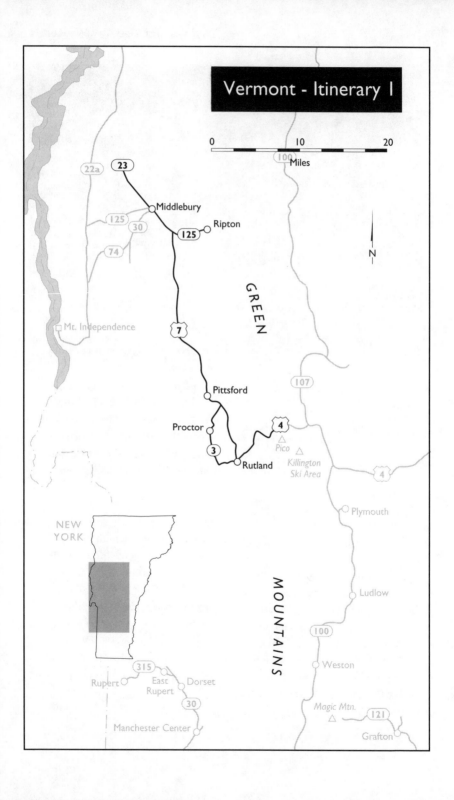

Vermont - Itinerary I

ITINERARY 1

Rutland • Proctor • Pittsford • Ripton • Middlebury

Rutland

Rutland, the second largest city in Vermont, was chartered in 1761 by Governor Benning Wentworth of New Hampshire. In the 1770s Rutland prospered as a frontier town, with both a gristmill and a sawmill. Later, the town and surrounding area became famous for its superb marble. The New York Public Library, the John F. Kennedy Memorial, and the Supreme Court Building were all built from marble quarried here.

Stop for a meal at *Sirloin Saloon* (Main Street, 802–773–7900) or *South Station* (South Main Street, 802–775–1736).

Proctor

To get a sense of how marble built the prosperity of the city, travel north on Route 3 to Proctor, the center of the marble industry. Head for the *Vermont Marble Exhibit* on the grounds of the *Vermont Marble Company* (800–427–1396 or 802–459–2300), several miles north of town. What's here? Samples of marble from all over the world, a view of the massive factory, a look at a sculptor at work, and movies that explain the quarrying process.

Between New York's Taconic Mountains and Vermont's Green Mountains, widening into Lake Champlain, lies the Champlain Valley. You can see marble in the rock all along the valley, where metamorphism—heat and pressure—has transformed the native limestone. Vermont is one of the largest producers of marble in the nation. The best commercial marble in the state lies on a north–south axis between Brandon and Dorset, and many of the quarries in the area—including the one in Proctor—are open for visits.

The town of Proctor was named for Colonel Redford Proctor, a descendant of Captain Leonard Proctor, who settled in Cavendish, Vermont, in 1780. Captain Proctor had a feud going with Salmon Dutton over Dutton's "turnpike," a toll road Proctor didn't see the need for. (In fact he built himself a "shunpike" through Middlebury—just to avoid paying Dutton's toll!) The family feud lasted seventy-five years, until Redford laid it to rest by marrying Emily Dutton in 1858.

From the town take West Proctor Road 1 mile south to **Wilson Castle** (802–773–3284). This thirty-two-room nineteenth-century mansion sits on 115 acres. In the house are stained-glass windows, furnishings from Europe and the Orient, and an art gallery.

Pittsford

Continue north on Route 3 and then Route 7 for about 4 miles into Pittsford. Here maple syrup aficionados will enjoy the **New England Maple Museum** (802– 483–9414). The museum houses a collection of antique sugaring equipment and a wall of panel displays that depict the development of the industry. There's also a ten-minute slide show about modern production methods. When you're through looking, step into the tasting area for a spoonful of fresh syrup!

Ripton

From Pittsford head north on Route 7, turning east on Route 125 to Ripton. Robert Frost lived here from 1939 until his death in 1963. His home, the **Homer Noble Farm,** is 2 miles east of the town. Through the years, the poet became involved in the Bread Loaf Writer's Conference at Middlebury College's summer campus, a few miles farther along Route 125. The **Robert Frost Interpretive Trail and Wayside Area** begins at the farm and ends at the Bread Loaf campus, which is located at the edge of Green Mountain Forest on Route 125. You can read seven of his poems on plaques along the way. Call the **Ranger District Wayside Area** (802–388–4362) for information and directions to Homer Noble Farm.

Middlebury

Return to Route 7 and head north to Middlebury, the home of **Middlebury College,** long noted as one of the best places in the U.S. to study foreign languages and literatures. Its lovely old Georgian and nineteenth-century buildings make this "college on the hill" just what a New England college should be.

One of our favorite stops in town is the **Vermont State Craft Center,** just off Main Street (802–388–3177). Here you'll find crafts exhibitions, classes, and wonderful collections of wooden toys, stained glass, jewelry, pottery, pewter, and more—all for the browsing or buying.

To reach the *Morgan Horse Farm* (802–388–2011), which is managed by the University of Vermont, head out Route 125 west to Route 23 and follow the signs. There is an audiovisual presentation about the farm and a tour of the stables.

FOR MORE INFORMATION

Addison County Chamber of Commerce, 2 Court Street, Middlebury, VT 05753; (800) SEE–VERMONT or (802) 388–7951; www.midvermont.com

Rutland Region Chamber of Commerce, 256 North Main Street, Rutland, VT 05701; (802) 773–2747; www.rutlandvermont.com

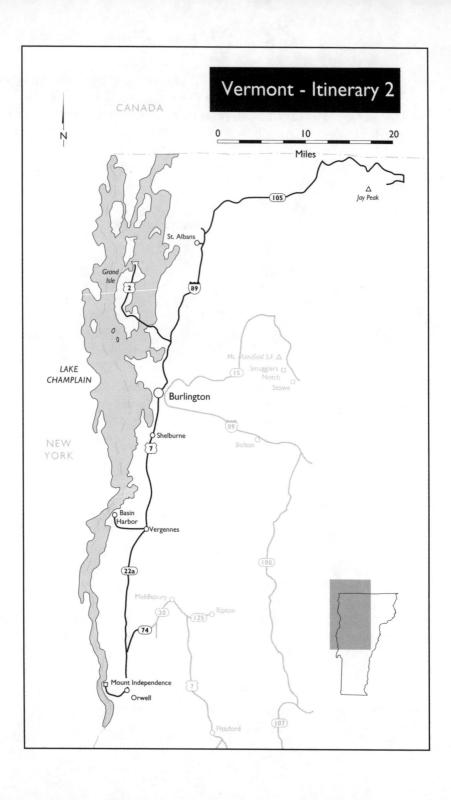

Vermont - Itinerary 2

CANADA

N

0   10   20
Miles

Jay Peak
105

St. Albans

Grand
Isle
2

89

LAKE
CHAMPLAIN

Mt. Mansfield S.F.
15   Smugglers
Notch
Stowe

NEW
YORK

Burlington

89

Shelburne
7   Bolton

Basin
Harbor
Vergennes

100

22a

Middlebury
30   125   Ripton

74

7

Mount Independence
Orwell

Pittsford
107

ITINERARY 2

Mount Independence • Basin Harbor
Shelburne • Burlington • Grand Isle

Mount Independence

From Middlebury, take Routes 30 and 74 west to 22A, then turn south to Orwell. *Mount Independence* (802–759–2412) was once the site of an important Revolutionary War military compound. In 1776, it was planned for a garrison of 12,000 men, the largest such compound in North America. A floating bridge provided access to Fort Ticonderoga. During the winter it became very difficult to send supplies there, so the force was reduced to 3,000 soldiers. By July 1777 the fort was taken by the British, who pursued the departing American troops, which led to the battle at Hubbardton. Today, remains include the blockhouse, gun batteries, a stockade, and a hospital. The visitors' center and museum display interactive exhibits featuring military artifacts. Bring your walking shoes and enjoy the trails within the park.

Basin Harbor

Head north on Route 22A toward Vergennes and turn left onto local roads signed for Basin Harbor. The *Lake Champlain Maritime Museum* (802–475–2022) offers a Revolutionary War gunboat replica, the *Philadelphia*. (The original is in the Smithsonian.) This vessel was one of Benedict Arnold's gunboats; it sank during the Battle of Valcour Island in 1776. Visitors can climb all over her, even help hoist a sail. Call ahead to be sure the vessel is in her home port.

The boat shop in the museum is the place to watch shipbuilders working on replicas. And a blacksmith continues to use his forge to make typical eighteenth-century boat fittings.

Shelburne

From Basin Harbor return to Vergennes and take Route 7 north to Shelburne. Here you will find the remarkable *Shelburne Museum*

(802–985–3346), with its extensive and varied collection of Americana. The thirty-seven buildings, spread out on forty-five acres of land, house collections of quilts, textiles, tools, glass, ceramics, scrimshaw, decoys, weathervanes, furniture, dolls, carriages, circus memorabilia, and wagons.

There are seven period homes; the oldest is the *Prentis House,* dating from 1733. Built in saltbox style, the house has a colonial kitchen with a large fireplace. This house contains seventeenth- and eighteenth-century furniture, decorative arts, and textiles. The *Dutton House* dates from 1782; it was moved from Cavendish, Vermont. The sawmill has an operating waterwheel and an up-and-down saw. The *Stagecoach Inn* was built in 1782 in Charlotte, Vermont. Visitors will enjoy the cigar store figures, weathervanes, whirligigs, and trade signs there.

The Shelburne Museum also includes a general store, a blacksmith shop, a schoolhouse, a church, a livery stable, an 1890 railroad station, a lighthouse, a smokehouse, the 220-foot sidewheeler SS *Ticonderoga*, a steam train, a railroad car, and galleries. Wear comfortable shoes (there is a shuttle bus for the foot-weary) and plan to spend the day.

Burlington

From Shelburne continue north on Route 7 into Burlington. It's the largest city in Vermont, both a university town and a city with a busy industrial area. The Chamber of Commerce (see below) or the Church Street Marketplace kiosk can provide background information on the city's cultural and recreational opportunities.

Burlington sits on the eastern shore of Lake Champlain, with several important harbors. The *Spirit of Ethan Allen* (802–862–9685) offers one- to three-hour cruises. Or you can take an hour-long ferry ride from the King Street Dock to Port Kent, New York. Call *Lake Champlain Ferries* at (802) 864–9804 for information.

On the water, keep your eyes open. There may be sea monsters in the lake! Way back in 1609, Champlain wrote about a creature he spotted that was 20 feet long, as thick as a barrel, with a head like a horse and a body like a serpent. In the 1870s "Champ" was sighted by hundreds of steamship passengers. And in 1977 a woman took a photograph of something that looks very much like "Champ." So watch closely!

Battery Park, on the waterfront at Pearl Street, was the scene of defensive shooting at British warships during the War of 1812. Today, you may sit back and enjoy the fine view of the Adirondacks across the lake. For swimming, picnicking, and camping, drive out North Avenue, to Institute Road, to *North Beach.*

Continue on North Avenue to *Ethan Allen Park,* part of the farm once owned by the fascinating leader of the Green Mountain Boys. Legends about Ethan Allen mix fact and fabrication. Once when he was walking through the woods a huge bobcat sprang and landed on his back; Allen reached behind and wrenched the cat onto the ground, then strangled it. When he arrived where he was going, he explained his delay by blaming the "Yorkers" for training and setting varmints against him. Another time he was said to have killed a bear by jamming his powderhorn down the animal's throat! Even a rattlesnake didn't get the better of Ethan Allen. One night after too much elbow bending, Allen and a friend stopped for a nap. A rattler coiled on Allen's chest, struck him several times, then rolled off, staggered, burped, and fell asleep. The next morning Allen complained about the pesky "mosquito" that kept biting him during the night.

Allen's drinking caused him some trouble at home, too. His wife, Fanny, finally worked out her own method for checking his sobriety. She pounded a nail high on the wall of their bedroom, In the morning, if she found his watch hanging on the nail, she knew he'd come home sober; if not, he was in for it. It didn't take Allen long to put one and one together. And after a while, no matter how much he was weaving about, he'd get that watch hooked on before he went to sleep.

When news leaked out of an impending real estate auction, Allen, his brother Ira, and the sheriff announced the sale would be delayed until one the next day. And it was—until one in the morning. Just after midnight the three men met. And at the stroke of one Ethan bid a dollar for the house, barn, and hundred acres; Ira bid two dollars; and the gavel fell.

For a glimpse into Allen's life, visit the *Ethan Allen Homestead* (802–865–4556) off 127 north. From the visitors' center you will walk past a garden blooming with plants grown by his wife. The path leads to his home. There's a four-poster bed in the living room with a straw mattress on a rope spring. Remember the phrase "sleep tight?" A twister-tool was used to make sure the ropes were tight.

Back in town, stop at the *Robert Hull Fleming Museum* (802–656–0750). There's an Egyptian mummy, a Kan Hsi vase, seventeenth-century Persian miniatures, and galleries with lots of exhibits. And if you're in Burlington between June and October, enjoy the *Mozart Festival.* Write ahead or call (802–862–7352) for a schedule of concerts.

Burlington offers gastronomic delights for everyone—in all tastes and price ranges. Try the *Ice House* (802–864–1800) on Battery Street, *Carbur's Restaurant* (802–862–4106) on Saint Paul Street, or *Sweetwater's* (802–864–9800) on Church Street. For terrific frozen treats try *Ben & Jerry's Ice Cream* (802–862–9620) on Cherry Street. Like to shop? Try the *Church Street Marketplace,* which features craft fairs and a sidewalk cafe.

Grand Isle

From the city take I–89 north to Route 2; then follow the signs across the bridge to Grand Isle. This quiet island is a wonderful place to relax. Three parks—*Grand Isle State Park, Knight Point State Park,* and *North Hero State Park*—offer swimming, boating, and camping. Contact the Department of Forests and Parks (802–241–3655) for information about them.

Valcour Island, on the west side of the lake in New York, between Port Kent and Plattsburgh, is where the first major naval battle of the Revolutionary War was fought, on October 11, 1776. In September of that year General Benedict Arnold assembled his naval forces between Valcour Island and the New York mainland. His fleet included the sloop *Enterprise*, the schooners *Royal Savage* and *Revenge*, and a number of smaller vessels. Captain Thomas Pringle led the British fleet—the schooners *Maria* and *Carleton*, and several dozen smaller ships.

On the first day the British held the advantage, then tried to maintain a line south of the island to hold the Americans in place. But in dense fog that night, the Americans sailed north around the island, then south all the way to Crown Point (16 miles north of Ticonderoga). Eventually, the British destroyed the American fleet, but General Arnold and his men escaped to Fort Ticonderoga. This battle upset British plans to capture the fort in 1776; instead they withdrew to Canada. In the meantime the Americans were able to strengthen their forces and were victorious at Saratoga in 1777, the turning point in the war.

Today, the island's 950 acres are uninhabited, preserved in their natural state. For bird-watchers there's a large rookery for great blue herons in the southeast corner; for hikers and campers there are 7 miles of trails and camping sites scattered around the island. For information, contact the *New York State Environmental Conservation Department* (518–474–2121).

Stop at *Allenholm Farm* (802–372–5566) in South Hero for apples (the island abounds with orchards), cheeses, jellies, and gifts. Driving along Route 2 you'll pass the **Hyde Log Cabin,** which is maintained by the Historic Preservation Department. Built in 1783, it is the oldest log cabin in the country.

When you're through exploring, you can follow Route 2 through North Hero and Alburg Center to Route 78 and Swanton, then Route 36 along the east shore of the lake, back to Burlington. Or if time is a problem, retrace your steps on Route 2 and I–89 into the city.

Side Trip–Jay Peak

Burlington is a good jumping-off place for ski country. If you'd like to try the northernmost ski area in Vermont head for **Jay Peak** (800–451–4449 or 802–988–2611). One way to get there is to drive I–89 north to St. Albans, then turn east on Routes 104, 105, 118, and 242. The vertical drop is 2,150 feet and lifts include a sixty-passenger aerial tramway, a triple chairlift, a quad, two double chairlifts, and two T-bars. Normally you can ski at Jay from early November to early May because it has the highest average annual snowfall (332 inches) in the East. This natural cover has helped Jay to develop extensive glade skiing in recent years. Now, of sixty-four trails, eighteen offer a wide range of glade experience.

Cross-country skiing is available at **Jay Peak Touring Center** (from outside Vermont 800–451–4449, or 802–988–2611 from inside Vermont), **Hazen's Notch Touring Center** (802–326–4708), and **Heermansmith Farm Touring Center** (802–754–8866).

If you're there during other seasons you can ride the **Jay Peak Aerial Tramway** for a view of four states and Canada from 4,000 feet up. The **Long Trail** (see page 31) crosses the summit of Jay Peak; hikers find the view worth the climb.  Fishing is available nearby in the Willoughby and Black Rivers, where you can expect to catch salmon, lake trout, rainbow trout, brook trout, bass, northern pike, and walleyes.

FOR MORE INFORMATION

Lake Champlain Regional Chamber of Commerce, 60 Main St., Burlington, VT, 05401; (877) 686–5253; www.vermont.org.

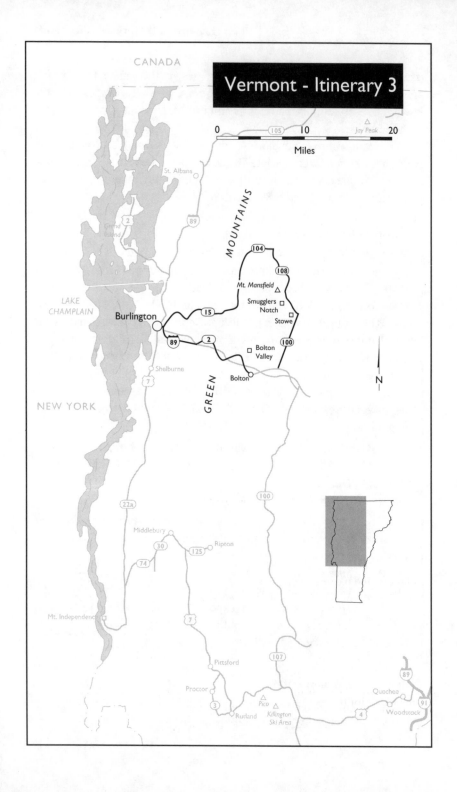

Vermont - Itinerary 3

CANADA

0   10   20
Miles

Jay Peak

St. Albans

LAKE
CHAMPLAIN

Burlington

Shelburne

NEW YORK

MOUNTAINS

Mt. Mansfield
Smugglers
Notch
Stowe

Bolton
Valley

Bolton

GREEN

N

Middlebury
Ripton

Mt. Independence

Pittsford

Proctor

Pico
Rutland   Killington
Ski Area

Quechee

Woodstock

ITINERARY 3

Smugglers' Notch • Stowe • Bolton Valley

Smugglers' Notch

Leave Burlington on Route 15, turn east onto Route 104 and south onto Route 108 to reach *Smugglers' Notch* (800–451–8752 or 802–644–8851).

How did a town in Vermont get stuck with a name that might have come from an adventure story by Rudyard Kipling or James Fenimore Cooper? There was no village until forty years ago, but the pass between Mount Mansfield and Madonna Mountain was called Smugglers' Notch in the first decade of the nineteenth century; its rugged topography suggests that it is just the sort of place real smugglers might like.

Smugglers' Notch ski terrain covers not one but three mountains: Morse at 2,250 feet, Sterling at 3,010 feet, and Madonna at 3,640 feet. Sterling and Madonna share the same base area, and Morse is linked to them by beginners' trails so anyone can ski back and forth between mountains. The vertical drop of 2,610 feet is among the highest in Vermont, and the three mountains provide sixty trails and 254 acres of skiing served by nine lifts.

The trails cover the whole spectrum of ability levels, from double black diamonds (even one triple black diamond) to beginners' slopes, with more than half rated as intermediate. The Nordic Center offers 23 kilometers of groomed and tracked trails. The village sits at the base of Morse, providing a multitude of services in a compact area—stores, lodging, restaurants, a fitness center, an ice rink, a tubing and sledding hill, sleigh rides, indoor and outdoor tennis, pools, a large day-care center, as well as crafts, classes, and parties for kids of all ages. It is no wonder that Smugglers' has been acclaimed as the best family ski resort in the country by a whole host of national magazines in recent years.

Smugglers' Notch is also a great place to vacation during the summer. Programs for young children are available at Alice's Wonderland winter and summer, with the addition of an outdoor pirate ship playground, petting zoo, and mammoth sandbox in warm weather. Discovery Dynamos is the place for three- to five-year-olds to explore the trout pond, have a look at a beaver dam, exercise their minds on treasure hunts, and enjoy water play. Adventure Rangers, for six- to ten-year-olds, offers team sports, swimming, treasure hunting, miniature golf, and water games. Notch Squad is for eleven- to fourteen-year-olds and offers science experiments, ice cream making, hiking, and swimming. Mountain Explorers, for adolescents ages fifteen through seventeen, offers watersliding, races on the Brewster River, and dance parties with disk jockeys.

While their kids are enjoying camp, parents can play golf or tennis, swim, learn how to flycast, ride horses or mountain bikes, enjoy fitness workouts, hike, canoe, or just relax. At the end of the day, they can cook in their condominiums or dine out right in the village. The staff will entertain children during "Parents Night Out."

Sight-seeing in the nearby towns and villages may include stops in antiques shops or a visit to the *Mary Bryan Memorial Art Gallery* (802–644–5100) in Jeffersonville, where Bryan's work is permanently displayed. A number of painters live in the Jeffersonville area, and the Northern Vermont Artists Association presents exhibitions during the summer.

Stowe

Just across the notch, of course, lies that old favorite, Stowe (800–253–4SKI or 802–253–3000), but during the winter you can get back and forth between the two resorts only on skis. Stowe is one of the closest major ski areas to Burlington: Take I–89 south until you reach Route 100 heading north to Stowe. Turn left onto Route 108 and the resort is 6 miles up on the left.

Dating from 1936, when it began with a rope tow, Stowe continues to expand and attract skiers from everywhere. With a history spanning close to seventy years, it is generally regarded as the queen of New England skiing. One of us still cherishes a silver medal earned on the Stowe Standard over half-a-century ago. The twin peaks, Mount Mansfield and Spruce Peak, offer enough variety to suit any family.

Mount Mansfield, at 4,393 feet the highest mountain in the state, looms over the surrounding countryside. There are several stories that explain the mountain's strikingly human look. One tells of a man named Mansfield who fell off Camel's Hump when the camel knelt to drink. He now lies face up, creating the mountain profile. Another legend says the profile is the face of Mishawaka, the son of an Indian chief, who crawled up to the peak to prove his courage and died there.

On Mount Mansfield, the ski area's vertical drop is 2,350 feet and the longest run is nearly 4 miles. The mountain boasts the first quad chairlift in the area, plus a gondola, triple chairlift, and two double chairlifts. Spruce Peak has 1,550 feet of vertical drop and is serviced by four double chairlifts. Altogether the two mountains offer forty-seven trails on 480 skiable acres with 73 percent snowmaking coverage.

Many people will want to take the eight-passenger gondola (the fastest in the world) to the *Cliff House* (802–253–3665) for a gourmet lunch, whether skiing or not. On a clear day there's a superb view of Mount Washington, not to mention the view of the cliff face right out the large windows. Alternatively, at the top of the Octagon Quad, you can eat at the *Octagon Quad Cafe* (802–253–3000) and enter cyberspace on one of its computer terminals, sending e-mail to envious friends at home.

Cross-country skiers have many areas to choose from at Stowe, including *Stowe Mountain Cross-Country Ski Area* (800–253–4SKI or 802–253–3000), *Edson Hill Manor* (802–253–7371), and *Top Notch Ski Touring Center* (800–451–8686 or 802–253–8585). You'll find that these trails interconnect, so you can really go out for a full day of exercise.

Many of us are delighted to catch a rerun of *The Sound of Music* on television; it is such a romantic story of a courageous family. After singing in concerts all over the United States for twenty years as the Trapp Family Singers, the Trapps began a new life as innkeepers in their Austrian lodge in northern Vermont. The original chalet burned in 1980—but the family's spirit is still here. *The Trapp Family Lodge* (800–826–7000 or 802–253–5719), nestled in mountains not unlike those in the family's native Austria, is located in Stowe, off Route 100.

If you're there in the winter you can cross-country ski on more than 40 miles of trails. (The same trails are available for walking during the warmer weather.) We suggest buying a waterproof trail map in the Trapp Touring Center and heading out for a few hours. Ski conditions are posted for each day, and trails are well marked. Those with stamina may want to ski the 5 kilometers to the Cabin for a bit of lunch or a snack. Or you can stop in the Austrian Tea Room, near the lodge, for a meal.

For those who've had a yen to try a health spa, there's one in Vermont: *Top Notch at Stowe Resort & Spa* (800–451–8686 or 802–253–8585). It's the perfect place for someone in a family who doesn't want to ski; even those who are staying elsewhere can come into the spa for a full or half day. Or you can choose to "SkiSpa," which involves skiing either downhill or cross-country for the morning and relaxing in the spa all afternoon. Guests can choose from a variety of services, including a fitness assessment, hydrotherapy treatment, skin care, water aerobics, and stress management, to name a few. To top it off, you can dine from a special gourmet menu and discreetly watch your calories.

You may not know that Stowe has been a summer vacation area since before the Civil War. Now you can reach the summit by riding a lift or driving your car on the Mountain Auto Road. Hiking in the mountains is popular, as are myriad summer sports.

Today, visitors can recapture some of the history of Stowe by taking a short walking tour around the center. Begin at the *Historical Society* (802–253–6133), then walk over to the brick *McMahon House,* built in 1855, on the corner of Main Street and Mountain Road; it was a station on the Underground Railroad, funneling escaped slaves to Canada before the Civil War. Farther along Mountain Road you'll see the *bridge* over the West Branch River. It was originally built as a covered bridge in 1848. Back on Main Street, notice that the *Masonic Hall,* built in 1890, has a "boomtown" facade; it was once a cobbler's shop.

The *Stowe Recreation Path* is a 5½-walking and biking path parallel to Mountain Road. Its entrance is along the driveway between the church and the hardware store. You can't miss the elegant *Stowe Community Church,* built in 1863, with a tall steeple that is the focus of most photographs of the town.

Hungry? There are more restaurants in Stowe than you can sample in one trip. Besides the ones mentioned earlier, some of our favorites are: *Charlie B's* (802–253–7355); *Fireside Tavern* (Stowe Mountain Resort, 802–253–3664); *Restaurant Swisspot* (Main Street, 802–253–4622); *Top Notch at Stowe* (in the Top Notch Resort—see above); the dining room in the well-known and loved resort, *Trapp Family Lodge* (42 Trapp Hill Road, 800–826–7000 or 802–253–8511); *Ten Acres Lodge* (14 Barrows Road at Luce Hill, 802–253–7638); *Edson Hill Manor* (1500 Edson Hill Road, 802–253–7371); *Mr. Pickwick's Polo Pub* (in Ye Olde England Inne on Mountain Road, 802–253–7558); *The Whip* (in Green Mountain Inn, Main Street, 802–253–7301); and *Gracie's Restaurant* (Main Street, 802–253–8741).

Shopping is available up and down Mountain Road. If you like *Moriarty* hats, stop in their shop on Route 100 (802–253–4052) to update yours or add a sweater or two. The range of colors and combinations is mind-boggling, but go ahead and choose! If you want to do more poking around the area, continue on Route 100 to *Cold Hollow Cider Mill,*

Waterbury Center (800–327–7537 or 802–244–8771) for fresh apple cider and more. Also in Waterbury you'll find the source of *Ben & Jerry's ice cream,* where you can take a *factory tour* (802–244–TOUR).

Bolton Valley

Even closer to Burlington than Stowe is *Bolton Valley* (802–434–3444). To get there, take I–89 south from Burlington to exit 11 (Richmond/Bolton exit) and go straight ahead onto Route 2 heading east for 8 miles. Turn left at the Bolton Valley Ski Area sign and follow the access road for 5 miles.

Bolton Valley was originally developed by the Des Lauriers family in 1966 after a land exchange for I–89 provided them with 8,000 acres of timberland. The family created an attractive year-round resort, with a special emphasis on preserving the natural beauty of the environment, and managed it for many years. Now under new ownership, the resort's slopeside lodging has been renovated, and the mountain has fifty-one trails on 168 acres of skiable terrain, with 60 percent of it covered by snowmaking.

Summer visitors can enjoy walking on the private nature preserve (where they may see a moose), hiking to the lookout, or just taking some quiet time to appreciate the view. Guests can participate in walking, hiking, tennis, swimming, and golf, take lessons in any of these sports, and work out in the sports center, which has indoor courts, a pool, and universal equipment.

FOR MORE INFORMATION

Smugglers' Notch Area Chamber of Commerce, P.O. Box 364, Jeffersonville, VT 05464; www.smugnotch.com; e-mail snacc15@hotmail.com

Stowe Area Association, Main Street, Box 1320, Stowe, VT 05672; (877) GOSTOWE or (802) 253–7321; www.gostowe.com

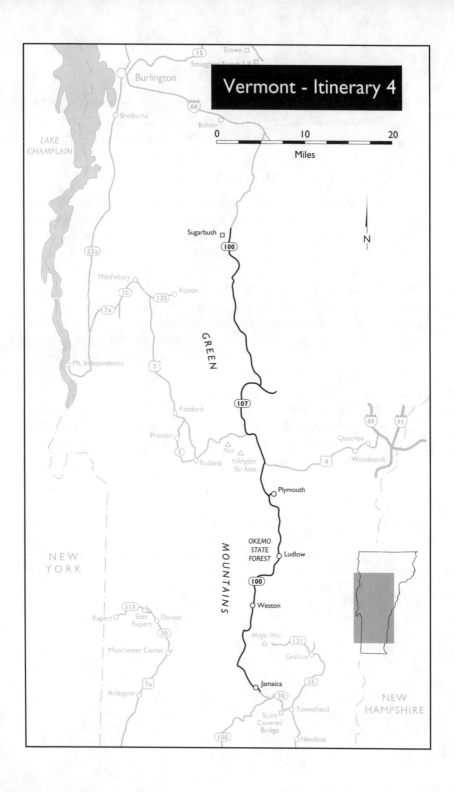

Vermont - Itinerary 4

ITINERARY 4

Sugarbush Valley • Plymouth
Ludlow • Weston • Jamaica

From the Mount Mansfield region, head south on Route 100, perhaps the most famous road in Vermont. It stretches all the way from Lake Mempremagog on the Canadian border to the Massachusetts border, following the spine of the Green Mountains much of the way. It's a great road to drive—almost an inventory of Vermont terrain—and you won't go far south before you come to the next major ski resort.

Sugarbush Valley

"Sugarbush Valley" is the generic name for the Waitsfield/Warren region. *Sugarbush* ski area (800–53–SUGAR or 802–583–6300), like Killington, is a compound resort; Sugarbush South Basin and Mount Ellen are now connected. The vertical drop is 2,600 feet. One hundred and fifteen trails flow from six interconnected areas, served by eighteen lifts and covering 468 skiable acres with 61 percent snowmaking coverage.

The most interesting of the high-speed lifts takes you not up one of the area's mountains, but between them, climbing up steep ridges and soaring over ravines in an exciting twelve-minute ride. Thus the link between Lincoln Peak and Mount Ellen, which used to be a road trip, doesn't require you to take your skis off. You zoom by the Wild Slide, a wilderness area open to expert skiers on guided tours.

Although Sugarbush is owned by the American Skiing Company and has the full range of amenities and services on the mountain, with seven new lifts and vastly increased snowmaking installed, it does maintain one Mad River Valley tradition in its Castlerock Peak area—purely expert terrain with no snowmaking and only occasional grooming. This is one of two havens for those who cherish skiing from the past, before heavy investment transformed the mountains. The other haven is part of an older, adjoining ski area, *Mad River Glen,* long famed as harboring the most difficult, narrow, twisting trails in the East. It still does, but the area, now owned by a cooperative, has also developed a full range of beginner and intermediate trails.

21

Over the years Sugarbush has acquired many images: meeting place for the jet set and New York fashion industry, training ground for serious racers and professional skiers, *après-ski* center for gourmet diners, and mecca for summer golf, tennis, and soaring enthusiasts. All of these descriptions reflect some truth about this multifaceted resort. Today Sugarbush still embodies the classic charm that has lured generations of vacationers. Thanks to a $35 million investment in lifts and snowmaking Sugarbush now combines modern amenities with pure Vermont charm.

The resort has cross-country skiing on site with 25 kilometers of groomed and tracked trails at *Sugarbush Inn* (802–583–2301). If you've wondered how Sugarbush got its name, just ski through the stands of maple and imagine them hung with buckets in early spring. More cross-country trails are available at nearby *Ole's* (802–496–3430) and *Blueberry Lake* (802–496–6687).

In the summer, *Camp Sugarbush* offers fun activities for kids, such as pony rides, swimming, nature hikes, and field trips to beaver ponds, fish hatcheries, and farms.

The Sugarbush area has lots of great places to have a meal, including *The Common Man* (German Flats Road, 802–583–2800); *Chez Henri* (Sugarbush Access Road, 802–583–2600); and *Warren House* (Sugarbush Access Road, 802–583–2421).

Plymouth

From Sugarbush continue south on Route 100 past Killington to Plymouth, where Calvin Coolidge was born in 1872. You can visit the President Calvin Coolidge State Historic Site, which includes the *Coolidge Birthplace* and the *Coolidge Homestead* (Route 100A, 802–672–3773 for both locations), where the president was sworn in. When President Harding died early in the morning of August 3, 1923, the news was carried from the main town of Bridgewater to the homestead by the telephone operator's husband—the Coolidges didn't have a phone! However, they did have a notary public handy for the swearing in— Colonel John Coolidge, the vice president's father. Someone later asked the colonel how he knew he could administer the oath of office to his own son. His reply: "I didn't know that I couldn't."

Ludlow

From Plymouth continue south on Route 100 into Ludlow. *Okemo Mountain Resort* (800–78–OKEMO or 802–228–4041), on your way into town, offers fine skiing in the winter and a general range of outdoor activities year-round.

For those who remember skiing Okemo years ago, as we do, the changes in the area will seem startling, but the development of the mountain has been carefully planned and executed. The vertical drop is 2,150 feet. There are now fourteen lifts, many of them triples and quads, serving ninety-eight slopes and trails on 520 acres of skiable terrain with 95 percent snowmaking coverage. In recent years Okemo has expanded in

both directions, to the south face on one flank of the mountain and to the Solitude area on the other. Now it is in the process of developing an adjoining mountain, Jackson Gore, which will provide another sixteen trails, as well as fifty-five acres of gladed trails. All this will be served by five new lifts, including a gondola. Additionally, Okemo has taken over management of Mount Sunapee in New Hampshire on a long-term lease.

If all of this seems to replicate the Killington story on a smaller scale, it doesn't. Okemo's owners, Tim and Diane Mueller, are both on the scene and active in managing the resort, and the image projected is that of an extended family rather than a corporate complex. Like Smugglers' Notch, this is an ideal destination for families and others who seek a mountain loaded with all levels of intermediate terrain.

When you're ready for a good meal on the Okemo slopes, head for *Gables* (800–78–OKEMO, ext. 1642), which is open for lunch. More casual spots on the mountain include *The Sitting Bull* in the base lodge, which serves Mexican fare plus soup and sandwiches, or *The Sugar House,* located on the lower slopes of the mountain, which offers salads and daily specials. *Willie Dunn's* (802–228–1387) serves lunch and dinner at the golf center.

Cross-country skiers can go across the road to *Okemo Valley Golf and Nordic Center* (Routes 103 and 100, 802–228–1396), which has trails along the river. Nearby *Hawk Inns and Mountain Resort* (Route 100, Plymouth, 800–685–HAWK or 802–672–3811) offers a large network of trails along the Black River as well as up on the mountain (see Appendix).

If you want to go out for dinner in Ludlow, try *Governor's Inn* (86 Main Street, 800–GOVERNOR) for gourmet cuisine with a flair (see Appendix), *Michael's* (Route 103, 802–228–5622) for seafood and steak, *Nikki's* (Route 103, 802–228–7797) for American regional cuisine, or *Echo Lake Inn* (Route 100, Tyson, 802–228–8602) for a "presidential dinner at an historic inn in Coolidge country." (See Appendix.)

Weston

From Ludlow follow Route 100 west to Weston, a charming village slightly off the main line. The *Farrar-Mansur House* (802–824–8190), Route 100, built in 1797, is just off the common. Once a tavern, it's now a museum. Nearby, the *Weston Playhouse* (802–824–5288) offers summer theater.

There are several interesting shops in the village. Our favorites are the *Vermont Country Store* (802–824–3184) and the *Weston Village Store* (802–824–5477).

Jamaica

Continue south on Route 100 through Londonderry to Jamaica, where white-water canoe and kayak championships are held each spring. Stop for a meal at *Three Mountain Inn* (Route 30, 802–874–4140). (See Appendix.)

FOR MORE INFORMATION

Sugarbush Chamber of Commerce, P.O. Box 173, Waitsfield, VT 05673; (802) 496–3409; www.sugarbushchamber.org

Ludlow Area Chamber of Commerce, P.O. Box 333, Ludlow, VT 05149; (802) 228–5830

Weston Community Council, P.O. Box 234, Weston, VT 05161; (802) 824–5606

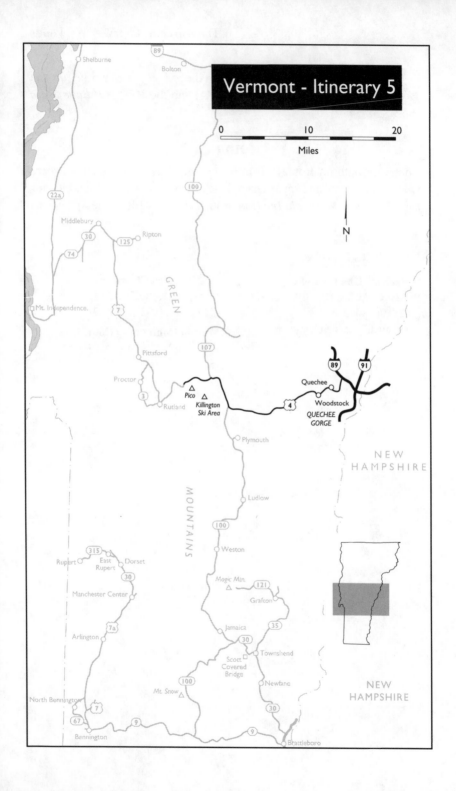

Vermont - Itinerary 5

Shelburne
Bolton
89

0   10   20
Miles

N

100

22a

Middlebury
30   125   Ripton

74

GREEN

7

Mt. Independence

107

Pittsford

Proctor
3
Pico △   Rutland   △ Killington
                        Ski Area

Quechee 89   91
        Woodstock
4   QUECHEE
    GORGE

Plymouth

NEW
HAMPSHIRE

MOUNTAINS

Ludlow
100

Weston

315   East
Rupert   Rupert
Rupert   30   Dorset

Magic Mtn. △
121
Grafton

Manchester Center

7a   Jamaica   35
Arlington   30

Scott
Covered
Bridge   Townshend

100   Newfane
North Bennington   Mt. Snow △
7   30
67
Bennington   9   9   Brattleboro

NEW
HAMPSHIRE

ITINERARY 5
Killington/Pico • Woodstock • Quechee

Killington/Pico

From Jamaica take Route 100 to West Bridgewater, where you will begin to meet the sprawling empire of ***Killington Ski Area*** (800–621– 6867 or 802–422–3333)—specifically, access to the Bear Mountain and Northeast Passage regions and, a bit farther on, the Killington Gondola. To get to the central region, continue around the mountain complex on Route 4 until you reach the Killington access road.

Killington Peak was the site of the christening of the state of Vermont. In 1763 the Reverend Samuel Peters and friends climbed to the top of Mt. Pisgah (later named Killington), carrying a bottle of champagne. When they reached the top, instead of enjoying a bubbly drink, Peters broke the bottle on a rock and christened it *Verd Mont* (French for "green mountain").

Killington is by far the biggest ski area in New England, stretching 11 miles over seven peaks from West Bridgewater to the west side of the Sherburne Pass, and now including the Pico ski area. Within this vast area there are 200 trails served by thirty-two lifts, including six high-speed quads, a two-stage "Skyeship" gondola, and another new eight-passenger gondola to the highest summit; 250 new tower snow guns cover 70 percent of the 1,182 acres of skiable terrain.

The connecting trails between Pico and Ram's Head will be completed in the near future. Killington has invested $60 million in mountain and base facilities during recent years, including the ***Killington Grand Resort Hotel,*** with the largest year-round conference facilities in Vermont. A full New England village between that hotel and adjacent base areas is also in the planning stage.

When you ski Killington you're not skiing just one mountain, but seven. Furthermore, they all interconnect by means of trails for all skiing levels. The vertical drop is 3,160 feet, and each peak and its area has its individual character. Snowshed is a slope for beginners, and Sunrise provides novices with long mountain runs, including the 10-mile Juggernaut. Intermediates can roam over most of the complex and will particularly enjoy Snowdon, Ram's Head, parts of Skye Peak, and much of Pico. Experts usually head for Bear Mountain, or the runs served by the Canyon Chair on Killington Peak or the Superstar Express on Skye Peak.

Lest you think that Killington is too big and complex to enjoy, remember that you will be skiing one area at a time, getting to know your favorite trails before moving on. You can stay up on the mountain most of the day, choosing trails that are less crowded rather than waiting in line at the bottom. Killington also boasts the longest ski season in the East and tries to be the first resort in the United States to open. If the temperatures are low enough, it usually succeeds, normally opening in mid- or late October and continuing until early or mid-June.

There's plenty to do even when the slopes are bare. Come in summer for golf, riding, or tennis. Snowshed hosts the Vermont State Craft Fair, Vermont Antiques Show, Vermont Gallery Showcase, and the Sportsman's Exposition.

Cross-country skiing is available nearby at *Mountain Meadows Ski Touring Center* (Route 4, 802–775–7077), which has 57 kilometers of groomed trails. They wander around Kent Lake and through the hemlock and white birch forest. The entrance road is located near the foot of Killington Road.

Many restaurants pop into view as you drive up Killington Road. Our favorites include *Charity's 1887 Saloon* (802–422–3800), *Choices* (802–422–4030), the *Grist Mill* (802–422–3970), *Mother Shapiro's* (802–422–9933), and *The Wobbly Barn Steakhouse* (802–422–6171).

And of course there's good hiking in this high mountain region. Try the *Deer Leap Mountain Trail,* which begins at Long Trail Lodge on Route 4 at the top of Sherburne Pass. You start out on a section of the mountain with fine views and rejoin Vermont's famous Long Trail, then you climb steeply to the south peak.

A word of caution: Don't head out on a trail with a guidebook as your only source of information. All hikers, regardless of their experience, need good topographic maps of the area they're exploring. U.S. Geological Survey maps are available at most local bookstores and stationery shops. Or you can call directly for them (800–USA–MAPS). *The National Survey* in Chester, Vermont (802–875–2121), is another source of good maps.

The *Bucklin Trail* to Killington Peak begins at Brewers Corners on the west face of the mountain and ascends through some old flat logging roads, then through some steeper rocks. It crosses Brewers Brook several times, winds in and out of Calvin Coolidge State Forest, then joins the Long Trail until it bears right, up to the peak. On a clear day you can see the Green Mountains stretching north from Pico Peak to distant Mount Mansfield, Glastenbury Mountain to the south, the Presidential Range to the east, and the Taconic and Adirondack Mountains to the west. To reach the trail, follow Route 4 to Mendon, then turn left onto Wheelerville Road. About 4 miles up the road you'll see a parking lot and the blue-blazed signs marking the path.

The *Long Trail* is a 263-mile footpath that stretches from Williamstown, Massachusetts, to the Canadian border near North Troy, Vermont. James Taylor, headmaster of Vermont Academy, came up with the idea for the trail in 1909. He organized a group of volunteers to clear a path linking the northern and southern peaks of the Green Mountains. His volunteers carried their equipment in pack baskets, clearing and building shelters as they went northward—a project that took twenty-two years. Today the trail is maintained by the *Green Mountain Club* (802–244–7037), which awards end-to-end emblems to those who walk the entire trail. (Over 2,500 have been presented.) There are sixty-five shelters along the way, each no more than a day's hike apart. The north end is marked by a marble monument, one side reading UNITED STATES, the other CANADA.

Woodstock

Continue along Route 4 to Woodstock, one of the loveliest towns in New England. Take time to walk around the green and enjoy the beauty of many authentic facades on the houses. Nearby, the *Woodstock Historical Society* (26 Elm Street, 802–457–1822) has nine restored rooms with collections of silver, glass, paintings, period furniture, and a landscaped garden. The house was built by Charles Dana in 1807. Don't miss the dolls and dollhouses, some belonging to local Woodstock families.

On Central Street, antiques shops, galleries, bookstores, and boutiques now occupy restored eighteenth- and nineteenth-century buildings. Don't miss the last covered bridge constructed in Vermont, located across the green from the Woodstock Inn.

Billings Farm and Museum (802–457–2355) is a wonderful destination for families. George Perkins Marsh, a linguist and diplomat, lived on the farm in the 1830s; his book *Man and Nature* reinforces the importance of what we now call ecology. Today the farm operates both as a dairy farm and as a museum. Life in 1890 on a Vermont farm is illustrated by exhibits about tasks such as clearing land, planting, threshing, cutting ice in winter, and making cheese and butter. Necessary tools and equipment are also on display. Jersey cattle, like the ones Frederick Billings bought in 1871, still win blue ribbons.

Restaurants abound in Woodstock. Our favorites include the *Woodstock Inn* (on the green, 802–457–1100), *The Village Inn of Woodstock* (41 Pleasant Street, Route 4, 802–457–1255), *Spooner's at Sunset Farm* (Route 4, 802–457–4022), *The Prince and The Pauper* (24 Elm Street, 802–457–1818), *Bentleys* (3 Elm Street, 802–457–3232), *The Jackson House Inn* (37 Old Route 4 West, 802–457–2065), and *Kendron Valley Inn* (Route 106, South Woodstock, 802–457–1473).

There is much to discover in this town, a town that has valued and preserved its heritage while adapting it to modern living. Contact the chamber of commerce (page 31) for more information about historic sites. It's the place, too, for information about nearby nature trails, *Faulkner* and *Mount Peg.*

John Freiden has written a wonderful book, *25 Bicycle Tours in Vermont*, and one of those trips begins and ends in Woodstock, with stops at South Pomfret, Hewetts Corners, and West Hartford. Bring the book and your bike for full enjoyment. Or if you'd like to join a group bicycle tour, contact *Vermont Bicycle Touring* (P.O. Box 711, Bristol, VT 05443; 802–453– 4811) or *Bicycle Vermont, Inc.* (P.O. Box 207, Woodstock, VT 05091; 800– 257–2226).

Woodstock is also a wonderful base for skiers who want to sample a variety of Nordic and downhill skiing. *The Woodstock Ski Touring Center* (800–448–7900 or 802–457–6674) is one of the most extensive in southern Vermont, offering 65 kilometers of skiing, with fourteen trails on the golf course and slopes of Mount Peg south of town and another eighteen on the uplands of Mount Tom, which overlooks the town from the west. Alpine skiers also have many choices within easy reach, starting with *Suicide Six* (802–457–6664) a few miles north of town. Woodstock was on the forefront of developing winter sports, and Gilbert's Hill, adjacent to Suicide Six, was the site of the first ski tow in America in 1934. With a vertical drop of 650 feet and twenty-two trails served by three lifts, it remains a low-key family ski area.

South of Woodstock, in Brownsville, is another classic ski area that a few years ago spent $3 million to add seven trails, expand snowmaking, and upgrade lodging units. *Ascutney Mountain Resort* (800–243–0011 or 802–484–7711), with a vertical drop of 1,800 feet and fifty-six trails served by six lifts, including a new high-speed quad from the base to the summit, provides 150 acres of skiable terrain with 95 percent snowmaking coverage. And for those who want to head for the higher mountains of Killington (now seven in all), the Gondola base is less than half an hour's drive from Woodstock.

Quechee

Quechee Gorge, Vermont's Little Grand Canyon, rises 165 feet over the Ottauquechee River. Stop for a good view of the gorge from the bridge on Route 4. Or hike along the *Quechee Gorge Trail,* which begins 0.3 mile beyond the gorge, near the state park entrance. Watch for the sign marked with blue blazes. The views along the trail are spectacular.

A favorite place to visit in Quechee is *Simon Pearce Glassworks* (802–295–2711) in a restored mill on the Ottauquechee River. Visitors are welcome to enter the workshop downstairs and see glassblowers at work. There's another Simon Pearce glassworks in Windsor (Route 5 north, 802–674–6280).

FOR MORE INFORMATION

Quechee Chamber of Commerce,
P.O. Box 106, 15 Main Street,
Quechee, VT 05059; (802) 295–7900
or (800) 295–5451

Woodstock Chamber of Commerce,
4 Central Street, Woodstock, VT 05091:
(888) 496–6378 or (802) 457–6674

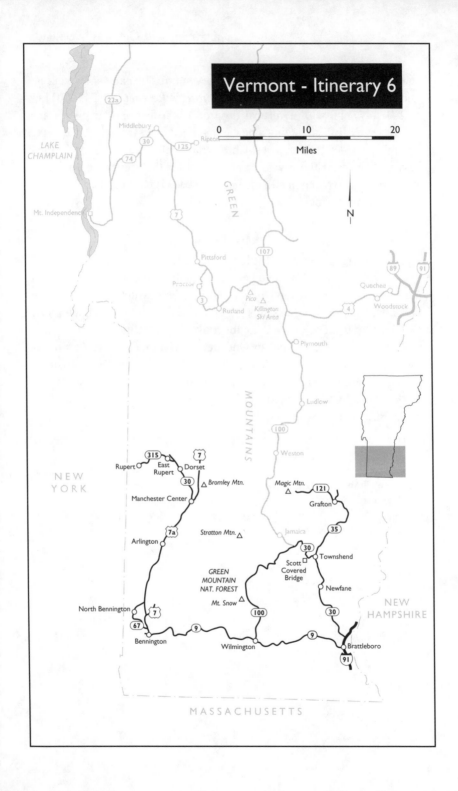

ITINERARY 6

Grafton • Townshend • Newfane • Brattleboro
Wilmington • Bennington • North Bennington
Manchester • Dorset/East Rupert

Grafton

Grafton is a lovely village, restored beginning in 1963 by the Windham Foundation. Money earned by businesses in town is plowed right back into the maintenance of the village. It looks very nineteenth-century, with nary a power line or utility pole in sight. Stop for a meal or overnight at the *Old Tavern at Grafton.* (See Appendix.)

The *Historic Grafton Information Center,* on Townshend Road (802–843–2255) is the place to go for lots of local information.

Tours of the *Grafton Village Cheese Company* (802–843–2221) are usually offered on Wednesdays, so call for a schedule. You can't miss the large round lazy Susan on the counter with all sorts of cheese to taste.

If you'd like to smell the fragrance of maple, plan to visit *Plummer's Sugar House* (802–843–2207) about the second week in March or thereafter. The sugar house is in full swing twenty-four hours a day during that time. However, you can buy Vermont maple products any time of the year.

Come to *Grafton Ponds* in any season to exercise and have fun hiking, biking, or skiing. There are 26 miles of ski trails to enjoy. One area is specifically for snowshoeing, and there's a hill for tubing.

Townshend

From Grafton head south on Route 35 to Townshend. Here you'll find the longest covered bridge in Vermont—*Scott Bridge*—spanning the West River. It was constructed in 1870 and extends 276 feet. In town, the 1790 *Congregational Church* is the archetypal New England church. It's also a favorite of jigsaw puzzle manufacturers—so you may already be familiar with it!

Newfane

Newfane, 4 miles south of Townshend on Route 30, is one of the loveliest towns in the state. The **Windham County Court House,** in Newfane Village Center, is a Greek Revival structure built in 1825.

Stop for a meal at the **Newfane Inn** (802–365–4427), right on Route 30. The inn is exquisite (it was built in 1787), and so is the food. Then walk across the street to the **Newfane Country Store** (802–365–7916). Its four rooms are filled with kitchen accessories, foods (the bread is delicious), quilts, and all kinds of country gifts. If you're looking for older treasures, come on a Sunday between May and October for the **Newfane Flea Market** on Route 30.

Brattleboro

Follow Route 30 into Brattleboro. It was the site of the first settlement in Vermont in 1724 at Fort Dummer. The town was once home to Rudyard Kipling. In 1892 the author married Caroline Starr Balestier. On her family's Vermont estate they built **Naulahka,** a home that Kipling described as a ship with the propeller (furnace) and kitchen at the stern, his study and a piazza at the bow.

It was here that he wrote *The Jungle Book, The Seven Seas,* and *Captains Courageous.* During a family quarrel over land rights, Beatty Balestier, Kipling's brother-in-law, made threats on his life. Balestier was arrested and Kipling moved to England. Today, you can see Naulahka from a distance, but it is not open to the public.

Wilmington

From Brattleboro, take Route 9 west toward Wilmington and watch for signs to **Molly Stark State Park** (802–464–5460). Molly Stark was the wife of General John Stark, who was called out of retirement during the Revolution to lead a thousand men across Vermont to protect munitions stored in Bennington. Stark wrote his wife: "Dear Molly: In less than a week, the British forces will be ours. Send every man from the farm that will come and let the haying go." She did as he asked and more; she sent 200 townspeople along, too. As he went into battle, General Stark said, "There are the Redcoats, and they are ours, or this night Molly Stark sleeps a widow." But she didn't. He won the battle and brought home a brass cannon, one of six taken from the British. (It's still on display in New Boston, New Hampshire, and is fired every Fourth of July.)

Return to Route 9 and turn north on Route 100 to **Mount Snow** (800–245–SNOW). For many years Mount Snow has offered wide smooth trails with the sun on them in the morning—the best way to encourage new and not-so-new skiers. We well remember the unique two-person gondolas that look like red, blue, or yellow eggs with skis hanging out the bottom. Over the years Mount Snow has become more sophisticated, even to the point of using computer-monitored snowmaking facilities.

Now a part of the American Skiing Company, Mount Snow added its **Grand Summit Resort Hotel and Conference Center** to its roster of base lodgings and recently invested $5.2 million in a new Discovery Center for beginning skiers and riders, as well as a hundred new tower snowmaking guns. With its companion mountain, **Haystack,** 2½ miles away, Mount Snow has a total vertical drop of 1,700 feet and 130 trails served by twenty-three lifts on 749 acres of skiable terrain covered by 85 percent snowmaking. The main mountain is almost completely served by snowmaking equipment, which makes beginning and intermediate skiers very happy.

In the summer, Mount Snow offers a 3-mile round-trip gondola ride to the top of the mountain, a golf school, tennis, swimming, horseback riding, sailing, windsurfing, and fishing. In addition, the area has many attractions such as antiques and flea markets, an air show, a music festival, and crafts fairs. For summer resort information call (802) 464–2151.

Bennington

Continue east on Route 9 to Bennington, the home of Ethan Allen's Green Mountain Boys, known as the Bennington Mob. On August 16, 1777, the Battle of Bennington was fought nearby (the actual battle site is near Walloomsac, New York). The battle marked a turning point in the war, weakening the British and forcing them to retreat. The **Bennington Battle Monument** (802–447–0550), a 300-foot-high obelisk built in 1891, commemorates General Stark's victory over the British, led by General John Burgoyne. If you're here in late August, you can witness the celebrations of **Bennington Battle Day Weekend.** Take an elevator to the top of the monument for a view of the countryside.

Farther up Monument Avenue, you can walk around Old Bennington and enjoy the lovely Colonial homes, the green, and **Old First Church.** This white clapboard structure has an unusual steeple with three tiers.

Inside, each of the six columns was developed from one tree. Vaulted ceilings and box pews complete this interesting period building.

Stroll through the *Old Burying Ground,* next to the church, to see the graves of five Vermont governors, the founders of Bennington, and the burial place of Robert Frost. His epitaph represents his life: "I had a lover's quarrel with the world."

About a mile beyond the center is the *Bennington Museum* (Route 9, 802–447–1571) and its collections of Bennington pottery, blown and pressed glass, paintings by Grandma Moses, costumes, and furnishings. The *Grandma Moses Schoolhouse* (802–447–1571), located next door to the museum, displays some of her paintings and mementos. Grandma Moses began painting at the age of seventy and continued until she died at 101. She lived on a farm in nearby Eagle Bridge, New York, and painted rustic landscapes.

Don't leave without stopping at *Bennington Potters* (802–447–7531) on County Street. You'll find a lovely gift shop and good buys on seconds.

North Bennington

Take Route 67 out of Bennington to North Bennington, where you'll find the *Park-McCullough House* (802–442–5441), a Victorian mansion furnished with period pieces. During the year, crafts fairs, art exhibits, square dances, and other events are held here.

Follow Route 7A north toward Manchester. Watch for the entrance to Skyline Drive, a steep narrow toll road to the top of *Mount Equinox.* The view from the 3,835-foot peak includes the spine of the Green Mountains, the backbone of Vermont and New York.

Manchester

Continue north on Route 7A and follow it into *Manchester Center.* The old town on the hill offers an impressive collection of stately Colonial homes. Robert Todd Lincoln built *Hildene* (802–362–1788), "hill and valley," in 1902 as his summer home. Furniture in the house came from five Lincoln homes, including his Chicago home, Mrs. Lincoln's parents' home in Mount Pleasant, Iowa, and that of a daughter and granddaughter.

Fortunately, Mr. Lincoln kept complete records of construction details, purchases, samples of wallpaper, and fabric. When restoration began in 1978, historians and restorers alike were able to make good use of them.

Visitors today will see the Aeolian pipe organ, which was purchased for Mrs. Lincoln in 1908, standing in the front hall. The original piano rolls are played for each set of visitors; 242 rolls are on the shelves beside the organ. Files in Lincoln's office still contain records from the Pullman Company, which he ran from Hildene during his annual six months' residence. His books, a press to make a second copy of correspondence, and a Densmore typewriter are just as he left them. Abraham Lincoln's stovepipe hat, along with a homemade hat box covered and lined with newspaper of the era, are in a glass case.

The gardens were restored through the Lila Acheson Wallace Fund. Their sculpted patterns are alive with color, perfect against the backdrop of the Green and Taconic mountain ranges.

The **Hildene Ski Touring Center** (802–362–1788) welcomes cross-country skiers during the winter. The Carriage Barn offers a warming place, and there are 15 kilometers of trails to enjoy.

The historic **Equinox Hotel and Resort** (800–362–4747 or 802–362–4700) is truly magnificent. The first hotel on the site was built in 1769; since that time historic events have swirled around it. A group of Ethan Allen's Green Mountain Boys met there just before the Battle of Bennington in 1777 and in 1863 Mary Todd Lincoln and two of her sons stayed at the Equinox. The hotel redecorated a suite of rooms in anticipation of a second visit from both President and Mrs. Lincoln in 1865, but he was assassinated a few months before the proposed visit. Visitors come from miles around to have a drink or light meal in **Marsh Tavern** or dinner in the dining room. The Equinox offers many year-round activities, including golf, fly-fishing lessons, and snowshoeing tours.

The Manchester area is filled with opportunities for outdoor activities: hiking, swimming, boating, and fishing. Fishermen everywhere know the town because the **Orvis Company** (802–362–3750) is located here. You can visit the famous producer of fishing equipment at their plant on Route 7A between Manchester and Manchester Center.

Spring is really on the way when the canoes start appearing on the Battenkill. The river flows south through the Vermont valley, between the Green Mountains and Mount Equinox. From the town square in Manchester, follow Union Street east about ¾ mile to the **Union Street Bridge**—your launching area. Oh, you may receive some glares from fishermen and leave a little paint on the rocks, but this river, with its very mild white water, is a joy to run. Where to stop? There's a campground

north of Arlington, and another near Shushan, New York—both good spots to end your trip.

The **Southern Vermont Art Center** (West Road, Manchester, 802–362–1405) offers art classes and concerts. Visitors enjoy the sculpture garden, Collector's Gallery, and the Botany Trail.

Don't leave town without stopping at the *Jelly Mill* (800–694–3494 or 802–362–3494) on Route 7. There are three floors filled with gifts of every description. When you've shopped to your heart's content, treat your stomach to lunch upstairs in the Buttery. Other recommended dining spots are the *Reluctant Panther Inn* (802–362–2568) for fresh seafood, quail, and lamb and *The Black Swan* (802–362–3807) for continental cuisine with a California flair.

At the junction of Routes 11 and 7A, stop and browse in one of the most complete bookstores anywhere—*Northshire Bookstore* (800–437– 3700 or 802–362–2200)—which has a stock appropriate to a major city bookstore.

If you're ready for skiing or hiking, head east on Route 11 to Bromley, or southeast on Route 30 to Stratton.

Bromley Mountain (800–865–4786 or 802–824–5522) has several distinctions, both as the resort in southern Vermont that collected scattered rope tows and first installed them on a single mountain, and as the only ski resort in the state that faces solidly south. That exposure proved a problem before the advent of snowmaking but now attracts many who are tired of skiing in the shade on cold winter afternoons. The resort has a respectable 1,334 feet of vertical drop and forty-two trails served by nine lifts, including two quads, on 175 acres of skiable terrain, with 80 percent snowmaking coverage. Aware of its heritage, the resort stuck to its own style in a major expansion of the base lodge.

During the summer, try the first and now longest alpine slide in North America. Ride up on the chairlift and then choose one of three tracks for your slide down to the bottom. You control the speed of your sled! Or you can choose to take the chairlift to the summit on weekends.

Nearby sits ever-popular *Stratton Mountain* (800–STRATTON or 802–297–2200), the highest mountain in southern Vermont, with an elevation of 3,875 feet. The Intrawest Corporation acquired the resort in 1994 and launched a $275 million makeover to enhance it as a premier four-season resort. For skiers, the vertical drop is 2,003 feet with ninety trails and ninety acres of glades in a total skiable terrain of 583 acres, 80 percent of which is covered by snowmaking. Of the twelve lifts, two are somewhat unusual—they consist of a six-passenger high speed chair and a twelve-passenger gondola to the summit.

One of the distinctive features of Stratton is the village, reminiscent of European alpine ski centers. The clock tower in the square is a good place to meet at the end of the day. Dating from the early 1960s, Stratton has attracted people who wanted to build second homes right next to the ski area. As you ski down the slopes you can glimpse one chalet after another waiting for their owners to come in after a day of skiing and put their feet up beside a roaring fire.

Stratton Mountain offers a number of restaurants within minutes of the village, if not right in it. *Liftline Lodge* (802–297–2600) is one. *Stratton Mountain Inn* (802–297–2500) offers meals in the Sage Hill Restaurant, a piano bar, and a cafe with live bands.

All summer long, you can play tennis and golf here. The *Stratton Sports Center* offers both summer and winter activities with fifteen outdoor tennis courts, three indoor tennis courts, three racquetball courts, a fitness center, a steam room, a suntan parlor, and a sports shop.

To explore the area north of Manchester, take Route 7 north to East Dorset. There's a fine area for hiking near *Emerald Lake State Park.* Instead of going into the park, bear right at the sign for *Natural Bridge.* Leave your car in the parking lot. The climb is steep, leading up to a deep gorge spanned at the top by a 2-foot-wide natural bridge.

Dorset/East Rupert

To continue your exploration of southern Vermont from Manchester Center, head northwest on Route 30 to Dorset. This charming village, with well-kept Colonial houses, was the site of the first marble quarry in the country. In fact, abandoned marble quarries are still scattered around. Visitors also come to fish for trout in the Battenkill River, Mettawee River, or Otter Creek. Others hike or cycle from inn to inn.

We can suggest a nice hike of less than 6 miles through beautiful country. Head up the hill from Route 30 on Hollow Road past lovely old homes to Kirby Hollow Road, where there is a beautiful yellow "Enfield" house. Take a right and, at the next fork, take another right onto Lower Hollow. You will be passing one pretty home after another, including saltboxes, Colonials, and a host of new contemporaries. The creek follows this road most of the way.

Continue on Lower Hollow for 2½ miles until you come to an old water mill and a large complex of white clapboard buildings. Turn left onto Upper Hollow Road and head back toward town. The views along this road of sloping meadows with gracefully curved patches of woods and mountains beyond are worth the walk. Then continue back to Route 30.

Church Street, just off Route 30, has one white house after another; all have either black or dark green shutters. Just beyond the church you can turn left onto Cheny Road to the ***Dorset Playhouse*** (802–867–2223), which is an established theater of professional caliber. Call for a schedule of performances. The Dorset Theater Festival has been going strong since 1976.

The Barrows House (800–639–1620), once a parsonage and now an inn, is the place to go for a gourmet dinner or a lighter meal in the tavern. ***The Dorset Inn*** (802–867–5500) is just what you have in mind when you think of an inn in Vermont. Stay for the night or just a meal in either place.

Continue north on Route 30 into East Rupert; then take Route 315 for 2½ miles, to the sign for ***Merck Forest*** (802–394–7836). This 2,600-acre forest, a treasure for hikers, was given to the town by George W. Merck in 1950. There is a year-round program of reforestation and logging, and signs at seven stations along the main trail describe the wildlife in the area. Before you start, register at the information booth and pick up a pamphlet. After Station 3 you come to a barn, the center of the educational program. There are a number of trails to follow, including the steep trail to Mount Antone, and there are nine overnight shelters that can be used with a permit. The forest is open all year and offers one of the finest cross-country ski terrains in Vermont.

FOR MORE INFORMATION

Bennington Area Chamber of Commerce, 100 Veterans Memorial Drive, Bennington, VT 05201; (802) 447–3311; www.bennington.com/chamber

Brattleboro Area Chamber of Commerce, 180 Main Street, Brattleboro, VT 05301; (802) 254–4565; www.brattleboro.com

Dorset Chamber of Commerce, P.O. Box 121, Dorset, VT 05251; (802) 867–2450; www.dorsetvt.com

Ludlow Area Chamber of Commerce, P.O. Box 333, Ludlow, VT 05149; (802) 228–5830

Manchester and the Mountains Regional Chamber of Commerce, 5046 Main Street, Suite 1, Manchester Center, VT 05255; (802) 362–2100; www.manchestervermont.net

New Hampshire

The Granite State

The first permanent settlement in New Hampshire was established in 1623 on Odiorne Point in Rye. Dover, Portsmouth, Exeter, and Hampton were settled soon after, and these five were the only towns in the area for years. Their isolation did not create good feelings among the settlements, and bitter arguments arose over land deeds and religion. Infighting was not the towns' only problem. At one point Massachusetts tried to take over the New Hampshire villages—a dispute that was settled by the crown in 1629.

Settlers in New Hampshire had to be persistent in their struggle to tame the rocky soil, clear forests, and cope with long winters. Although they had a good relationship with Native Americans in the beginning, eventually their lumbering and construction encroached upon tribal lands and rights. Finally, in 1675, King Philip's War erupted as a protest against the settlers. The Wampanoags, Narragansetts, and Nipmucks joined forces under the chief of the Wampanoags, Philip (Metacomet). For one year they raided settlements with great loss of life on both sides. As time passed, the settlers learned to use the resources around them. Fisheries grew up along the shore, including the processing of salt cod. The tall pines of New Hampshire, some rising to 200 feet, were harvested and used as masts for English ships. But eventually, as their own shipbuilding began, the settlers were not happy to see the very best of the lot marked with the king's broad arrow and shipped off to mast the British fleet.

John Wentworth, chosen by the king in 1717 to govern New Hampshire, was a capable leader who provided stability for the settlers. Benning Wentworth, appointed governor of New Hampshire in 1741, was more controversial. He granted tracts of land to people, keeping 500 acres from each tract for himself, as well as charging a fee for each transaction. Later his grants west of the Connecticut River led to lengthy disputes with New York, which claimed the same land; they were finally resolved only when Vermont became a state in 1783. His nephew, John Wentworth II, carried on the family leadership as a royal governor until 1775, when he fled from a threatening mob in Portsmouth.

New Hampshire was the first of the colonies to declare its independence from England, with its own government taking power on January 5, 1776. "Live free or die," words written by General John Stark, New Hampshire's Revolutionary War hero, now are known as the state motto.

New Hampshire's White Mountains are extremely rugged and irregular, in sections resembling the Rockies more than any other mountains in the East. Once much taller, these mountains have been ravaged by periods of folding, faulting, and terrific pressure from molten rock within them. What this has done is create a landscape cut by ravines and embellished with unusual contours.

ITINERARY 7
Hampton Beach • Portsmouth

New Hampshire's shape is close to triangular, with a bulge near the base taking up little space along the New England coast. This itinerary is short because the shoreline area is an interlude of only 18 miles between the coasts of Massachusetts and Maine—but that short stretch is lined with beautiful ocean beaches.

Hampton Beach

If you come across the border from Massachusetts leave the New Hampshire Turnpike (I–95) and follow Route 1A along the coast to Hampton Beach. Here you can stop for a swim in the ocean, a stroll along the boardwalk, or a waterslide ride. From Hampton Beach harbor you can board a boat for deep-sea fishing or whale watching. More activity? There's often a talent show, a fishing derby, or a regatta going on in this busy resort town.

Portsmouth

Continue up Route 1A through Rye Beach into Portsmouth, New Hampshire's historic seaport that fueled the city's early affluence. Portsmouth is also a service center for the ***Portsmouth Naval Shipyard*** across the river in Kittery, Maine.

Imagine the delight of the first settlers when they disembarked from the *Pied Cow* and found wild strawberries growing in great profusion along the banks of the Piscataqua River. They named their settlement "Strawbery Banke," which lasted until 1653 when it was renamed Portsmouth. Strawbery Banke prospered as a deepwater seaport, fishing center, shipbuilding site for clippers, and lumber depot.

You might begin your visit at Portsmouth's major historical museum, aptly-named ***Strawbery Banke*** (Marcy Street, 603–433–1100), located in the "Puddle Dock" section of town. Rather than allowing their many surviving historical buildings to be razed, determined inhabitants began a major restoration in the late 1950s.

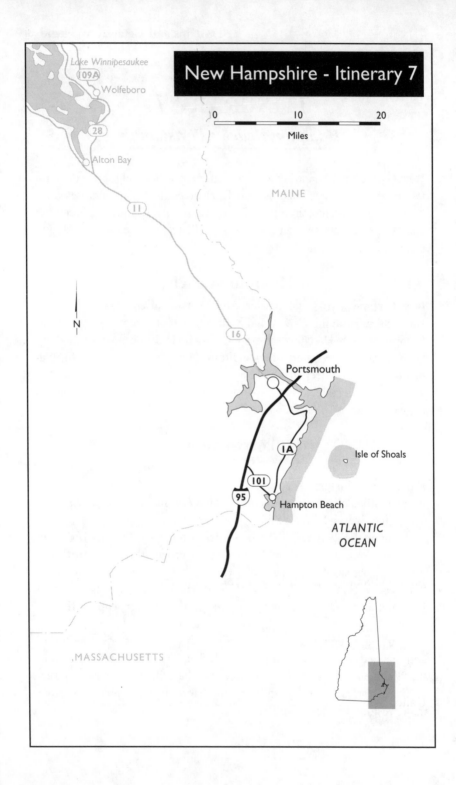

New Hampshire - Itinerary 7

Put on your walking shoes and, at the entrance, pick up a map that will introduce you to a tour of thirty-five historic buildings. You can wander in and out of a wide range of structures, including the elegant *Governor Goodwin Mansion* and the *Dinsmore Shop,* where the museum's cooper makes barrels. The *Goodwin Garden* has a Victorian flair, and the *Joshua Jones House,* dating from 1790, contains an archeological laboratory from the "digs" on the grounds of the museum. Part of the fun is seeing restoration still going on as building after building is readied for visitors.

Pitt Tavern, built in 1766, was visited by George Washington, the Marquis de Lafayette, and John Hancock, among others. It was also a stage stop with a constant flow of travelers arriving with fresh news.

Across the street, on the bank of the river, is *Prescott Park.* Come in the summertime to enjoy the beautiful flower gardens, free outdoor concerts, and arts and crafts exhibits.

The Historic Associates of the Greater Portsmouth Chamber of Commerce maintains old homes in town and keeps them open. Your map will show you the way to all of them along the historic *Portsmouth Trail.* The *Moffatt-Ladd House* (154 Market Street, 603–436–8221) was built in 1763 as a wedding gift for Samuel Moffatt from his father, an English sea captain named John Moffatt. John's son-in-law, William Whipple, a signer of the Declaration of Independence, later lived here. There are three floors of eighteenth-century furnishings, a cellar with a secret passageway to the wharves, and beautiful terraced gardens.

The *John Paul Jones House* (43 Middle Street, 603–436–8420) served as Jones's home while he supervised the outfitting of the *Ranger* in 1777 and the *America* in 1781. The house was built by Captain Purcell, who lived there with his wife Sarah, niece of Governor Benning Wentworth. After Purcell's death in 1776, Sarah took in boarders, and John Paul Jones is the one most remembered today. The house contains eighteenth-century furniture, cookware, silver, glass, ceramics, portraits, guns, and a wooden leg—not an uncommon aftermath of naval warfare.

The *Governor John Langdon House* (143 Pleasant Street, 603–436–3205) was built in 1784 and contains beautiful carvings. George Washington visited the house in 1789 and wrote about both the house and his host with compliments. John Langdon was a prominent statesman and patriot, both governor of New Hampshire and later the first president of the United States Senate. His fortune came from shipbuilding and privateering during the Revolution.

Another Georgian mansion, the **Wentworth Gardner House** (50 Mechanic Street, 603–436–4406) was built in 1760 for Thomas Wentworth, brother of John Wentworth II, the last of the royal governors. Look for the windmill spit in the great fireplace in the kitchen, Bristol tiles in blue or mulberry around most of the fireplaces, hand-painted Chinese wallpaper in the north parlor, and French wallpaper in the dining room.

The **Warner House** (150 Daniel Street, 603–436–5909) was built in 1716 for Captain Archibald MacPhaedris from brick carried as ballast in the hold of his ship. Original painted murals are still in place on the staircase. Look for the two murals on the stair landing that portray the American Indians who were taken to London to meet Queen Anne in 1710. The lightning rod on the west wall may have been installed under the watchful eye of Benjamin Franklin in 1762.

If you've never been aboard a submarine before, you can have that chance in Portsmouth. The USS *Albacore* (Albacore Park, 603–436–3680), built in the Portsmouth Naval Shipyard in 1952, was in active service from 1953 to 1972. She is 205 feet long, has a maximum speed of over 20 knots, and carried a crew of fifty men and five officers. Those who thought that she should be returned to her birthplace had their work cut out for them during two years of planning and coping with mountains of paperwork.

In April 1984 she was towed to Portsmouth, where preparations were made to bring her into drydock. It wasn't easy—a railroad bridge had to be

Side Trip–Isles of Shoals

In Portsmouth, board the *Thomas Laighton*, a schooner run by the *Isles of Shoals Steamship Company* (Market Street Dock, 800–441–4620 or 603–431–5500), and cruise to the Isles of Shoals. The islands, which lie 8 miles out of Portsmouth Harbor, were discovered in 1614 by Captain John Smith. They were a prosperous fishing center until the Revolution, when most of the residents moved to the mainland.

Star Island still maintains a little stone chapel more than 150 years old and a graveyard supposedly hiding pirate treasure. Or is the treasure on Appledore Island? Rumor has it that Captain Kidd killed one of his men here so that he would haunt (and guard) the spot where the treasure lies. "Old Bab" has been seen, with white face and a ghostly light emanating from his body, wearing a red ring around his neck.

taken apart, a dual highway cut through—and the project came to a standstill while she sat looking "like a beached whale." Finally, creative minds built a series of locks, and the 1,200-ton sub was floated onto her concrete cradle in Albacore Park. As you walk through, ask yourself if you would have felt claustrophobic while under the sea for long periods of time.

Hungry? There are lots of good restaurants in town. Our favorites: *Dolphin Striker* (15 Bow Street, 603–431–5222) and *The Library* (401 State Street, 603–431–5202).

From Portsmouth, you have a choice of traveling to southern or northern New Hampshire or heading into Maine. If you're going to southern New Hampshire take I–95 south to the Exeter Hampton Expressway and Route 101 through Manchester (I–293 bypass), to join Itinerary 9 or 10. If you're going to the lake district, drive northwest on the Spaulding Turnpike (Route 16), then take Route 11 to the Lake Winnipesaukee region (Itinerary 8). The route from Portsmouth to northern New Hampshire for Itineraries 12 or 13 begins on the Spaulding Turnpike and then continues north on Route 16 to Conway. To head into Maine and join Itinerary 16, take I–95 north across the river to Kittery.

FOR MORE INFORMATION

Hampton Beach Area Chamber of Commerce, 490 Lafayette Road, Box 790, Hampton, NH 03842; (603) 926–8717; www.hamptonbeach.org

Portsmouth Chamber of Commerce, 500 Market Street, Portsmouth, NH 03802; 603–436+1118; www.portcity.org

Old Bab may not be real, but the treasure was. In the early 1800s Captain Haley found silver bars on Smuttynose Island while he was digging a well. Haley, who owned a mill and a ropewalk, kept a lighted lamp in the window for ships at sea. In 1813 the *Sagunto* foundered off the island. Three survivors crawled toward his light in vain and they were buried on the island. (Look for the gravestones near the mill.) Smuttynose saw more tragedy in 1873, when Louis Wagner rowed out to search for treasure and killed two of the three women living on the nearly deserted island. The survivor, Maren Hontvet, escaped to tell the horrible story. The well where Wagner tried to wash the blood from his hands is still here.

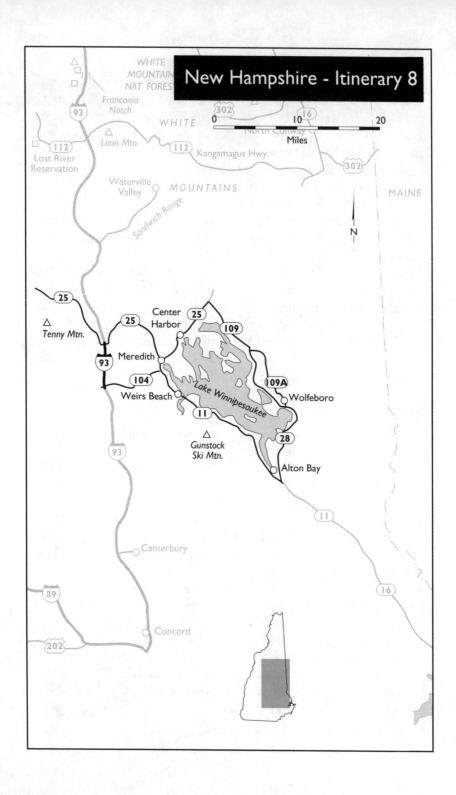

New Hampshire - Itinerary 8

ITINERARY 8

Wolfeboro • Weirs Beach • Meredith • Center Harbor

Lake Winnipesaukee is New Hampshire's largest lake, covering 72 square miles and 183 miles of shoreline. Native Americans gave it an appropriate name that means "the smile of the Great Spirit." Formed by glaciers, the lake is dotted with 274 islands (a number of them occupied by summer residents and campers) and is ringed by three mountain ranges. On a clear day, there are spectacular views of Mount Washington from some parts of the lake.

This itinerary begins at the southeastern end of the lake in Wolfeboro, reached by branching off Route 11 and heading northeast on Route 28.

Wolfeboro

Wolfeboro claims to be the oldest summer vacation resort in the country. In 1768 Governor John Wentworth came up from Massachusetts to build a summer home here; it burned in 1820, but many more lovely homes have been built since. Stop for a meal at the *Wolfeboro Inn* (603–569–3016) on North Main Street. And if you have time for some scenic touring, take a drive up the east shore of the lake on Route 109.

Weirs Beach

On the western side of the lake, there is another scenic drive from Alton Bay at the foot of the lake to Glendale on Route 11. A bit farther north, *Weirs Beach* offers good swimming, sailing, fishing, waterskiing, and a boardwalk. The best way to see the lake is to get on it, either by renting a boat or taking a three-hour cruise on board the *M/S Mount Washington* (888–843–6685), which leaves from Weirs Beach. Or for a closer look at the islands you can choose to ride with the mail on the *M/V Sophie C* (603–366–5531) as she makes her dockside stops around the lake.

Meredith

Not far north along the west shore you will reach Meredith, located between Lake Waukewam and the head of a northwestern bay on Winnipesaukee. That site made it a perfect spot for the early development of industry, with a waterway between the two lakes providing power for mills. John Jenness bought water rights and land in 1795 and then built a gristmill and a sawmill on the waterway. Later, John Bond Swasey channeled the water under the Main Street horse path and over a 40-foot waterfall. He used the power from this source to saw lumber, grind flour, comb cotton flax, and weave cloth.

Although fire and bad times destroyed and closed the mills, a few of their buildings remain, and they have been converted to contemporary uses. The *Mill Falls Marketplace* (603–279–7006) is housed in one of the old mill buildings, reconstructed and renovated, surrounded by inns, restaurants, and other amenities for visitors. Stop for lunch or dinner at *Mame's* (603–279–4631) or at the *Boathouse Grille* (603–279–2253) on the waterfront.

Center Harbor

Center Harbor, at the northern end of the lake, is a resort community located between the big lake and Squam Lake. If you loved *On Golden Pond* you can visit the actual setting for the film—*Squam Lake* in nearby Holderness. You can explore this quieter lake on a pontoon boat with the

---

Side Trip–Skiing in the Winnipesakee Region

If you are visiting the Lake Winnipesaukee region during the winter months, two downhill ski areas—each with a more than respectable vertical drop of 1,400 feet—are close at hand. Just off the west shore in Gilford, *Gunstock* (Route 11A, 603–293–4341) has eight lifts and forty-five trails, a total of 220 skiable acres with 80 percent snowmaking coverage. Northwest of the lake, in Plymouth, *Tenney Mountain* (Route 3A, 603– 536–4125) has four lifts and thirty-three trails, a total of ninety skiable acres plus three glades, with 90 percent snowmaking coverage on the trails. For cross-country skiers, Gunstock has 50 kilometers of trails and *Nordic Skier* in Wolfeboro (Route 28⁄109, 603–569–3151) has 40 kilometers. At both of these areas, snowshoers may use the cross-country trails and explore the backcountry.

Original Golden Pond Tour (603–279–4405) or just settle yourself on the shore and listen for the mournful call of the loons.

For a spectacular view overlooking Winnipesaukee, head east of Center Harbor on Route 25 through the center of Moultonborough and turn southeast on Routes 109 and 171. Keep going until you see signs for *Castle in the Clouds* (800–729–2468), mountainside site of Castle Springs, bottlers of spring water and brewers of local beer. There you can gaze at the lake from the snack shop patio, ride a tram to the spring, and take guided horseback rides on mountain trails.

For those who always want to see what's beyond the next bend of the trail or turn in the road—and that describes one of us quite exactly—completing the circuit of Winnipesaukee may be in order. To do that, head south from Moultonborough on Route 109 for a pleasant drive back to where we began at Wolfeboro. If you are heading for the White Mountains, stay on Route 25 from Moultonborough to West Ossipee and drive north on Route 16 to Conway.

If you are headiing for northern New Hampshire, take Route 25 east to Route 16 north and continue through Conway to join Itinerary 12 at North Conway. If, on the other hand, you are heading for southern New Hampshire, take Route 25 west and Route 3 south to I–93 south. At exit 14, take Routes 202 and 9 west, where you will join Itinerary 9.

FOR MORE INFORMATION

Greater Laconia/Weirs Beach Chamber of Commerce, 11 Veteran's Square, Laconia, NH 03246; (800) 531–2347 or (603) 524–5531; www.laconia-weirs.org

Lakes Region Association, P.O. Box 430, New Hampton, NH 03256; (800) 60–LAKES or (603) 744–8664; fax (603) 744–8659; www.lakesregion.org

Meredith Chamber of Commerce, Meredith, NH 03253; (603) 279–6121; www.meredithcc.org

Wolfeboro Chamber of Commerce, Wolfeboro, NH 03894; (800) 516–5324 or (603) 569–2200; www.wolfeboro.com/chamber

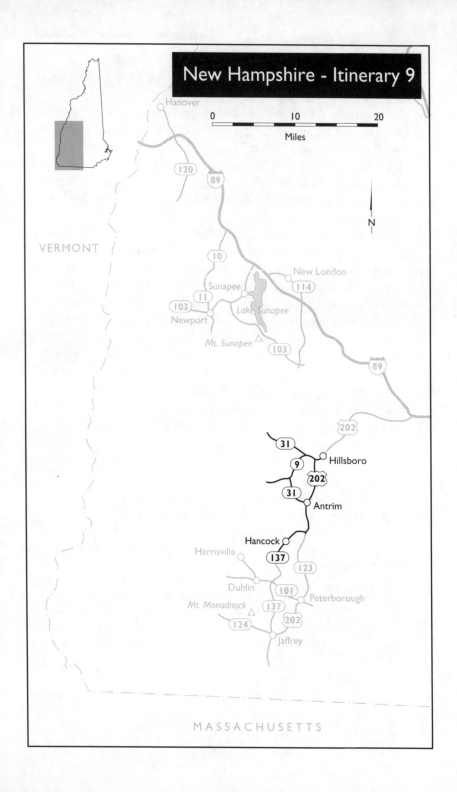

New Hampshire - Itinerary 9

0   10   20
Miles

N

Hanover

VERMONT

120
89

10

New London

Sunapee
114

11
103

Newport
Lake Sunapee

Mt. Sunapee
103

202

31

9
Hillsboro

202

31

Antrim

Hancock
137

Harrisville
123

Dublin
101

Peterborough

Mt. Monadnock
137

124
202

Jaffrey

MASSACHUSETTS

ITINERARY 9
Hillsborough • Antrim/Hancock

Apart from the brief coastal plain, so much of New Hampshire is mountainous that small agricultural communities in the state tended to remain isolated and self-sufficient throughout the eighteenth and early nineteenth centuries. During the second half of the 1800s, however, as industry swept into the state and rivers provided power for mills, cities like Manchester and Concord grew. Some of these mill towns still flourish, while most have turned to different kinds of industries to survive. As in neighboring Vermont, much of New Hampshire's economic development in recent years has been built on tourism. And southern New Hampshire is an extremely pleasant and easily accessible vacation area, with mountains, lakes, and forests to entice its visitors.

Hillsborough

The *Franklin Pierce Homestead* (Junction of routes 9 and 31, 603–478–3165) was built in 1804 by Benjamin Pierce, a general in the American Revolution and two-time governor of New Hampshire. His son, Franklin Pierce, was the fourteenth president of the United States, from 1853 to 1857. This white Colonial center-chimney home with green shutters is maintained by the Hillsboro Historical Society.

Antrim/Hancock

From Hillsborough continue south on Routes 9 and 31 through rolling hills past *Franklin Pierce Lake* to Antrim. The town was originally settled by Scots who had landed in Ireland in the seventeenth century and then crossed the Atlantic in the early eighteenth century, as one of our ancestors did. To reach Hancock follow Routes 31/202 past Bennington and take Route 137 into Hancock, which has an exceptionally attractive Main Street with large homes dating from 1781. The bell in the *Town Meeting House* was cast by Paul Revere and his son. Look for the *Harris Center for Conservation Education* (King's Highway, 603–525–3394), which was created to introduce people to the forests, lakes, meadows, monadnocks (hills and mountains of hard rock that resist erosion), and wildlife of the area. The center offers programs to schools and the public. If you're around on Halloween, you might learn to carve "mangel-wurzels," the ancient Celtic predecessors of jack o' lanterns.

For More Information

Hillsborough Chamber of Commerce, Hillsborough, NH 02344; (603) 464–5858

ITINERARY 10

Peterborough • Jaffrey/Rindge
Mount Monadnock • Dublin

Peterborough

Here you can see the outside of the home of composer *Edward MacDowell,* now the home of the *MacDowell Colony* (603–924–3886). Writers, painters, sculptors, composers, and filmmakers come as resident artists to create their works, undisturbed by anyone. You can visit MacDowell's grave, the library, and Colony Hall, and you might see an artist or two who have been working hard all day out stretching their legs or attending the theater.

Peterborough Players (603–924–7585) offer summer theater off Middle Hancock Road at the Stearns Farm.

Jaffrey/Rindge

Take Route 202 to Jaffrey and drive onto *Jaffrey Center.* It is filled with lovely large white buildings, including a 1775 meeting house which was raised on the day of the Battle of Bunker Hill.

Now head east on Route 124 toward New Ipswich, and turn right on Prescott Road just before the Millpore factory. The road travels into Rindge, where you will come to *Cathedral of the Pines* (603–899–3300), an outdoor shrine dedicated to the memory of the son of Dr. and Mrs. Douglas Sloane. A bell tower contains a carillon and two large Sheffield bells. The Altar of the Nation has a stone from each of our states to honor all of America's war dead. Services are conducted for those of all faiths,

Side Trip–Harrisville

Take a side trip to Harrisville by turning north onto New Harrisville Road, near *Yankee Magazine* headquarters. Harrisville is one of the most perfectly preserved New England mill villages to be found anywhere. Brick buildings are grouped along the pond and river. Look for the series of gates letting water cascade down the millrace all through the town.

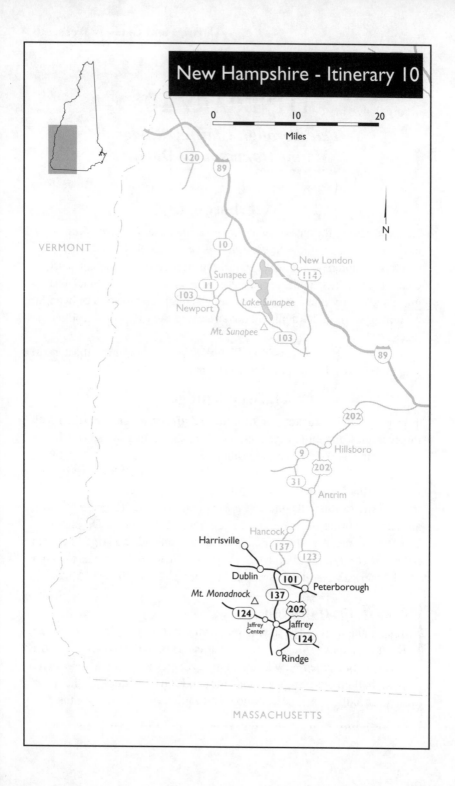

New Hampshire - Itinerary 10

0   10   20
Miles

VERMONT

N

120
89

10

New London
Sunapee   114
11
103   Lake Sunapee
Newport
Mt. Sunapee   103

89

202

9   Hillsboro
202
31
Antrim

Hancock
137
123

Harrisville
Dublin   101
Mt. Monadnock   137
124   202   Peterborough
Jaffrey
Jaffrey   124
Center
Rindge

MASSACHUSETTS

and there are outdoor chapels and flower gardens to visit. Imagine attending a service under the whispering pines, sitting on benches over a pine-needle floor, and looking out over the hillside to Mount Monadnock and into the vast space beyond.

Mount Monadnock

Hikers, we're coming to you. Like skiing in Tuckerman's Ravine on Mount Washington, climbing Monadnock is a New England ritual, almost a rite of passage for the young. We remember our own eager children, with others in a group of neighbors, racing ahead on the trail so fast that the parents couldn't keep up with them.

From Jaffrey head north on Route 124 for *Monadnock State Park* (603–532–8862). Continue on to the main gate where you can get trail maps; there are many trails up to the top. For a three- or four-hour hike up a reasonably steep trail, take *White Dot* or *White Cross* trails. For an easier five- to seven-hour climb, try *Cascade* to *Pumpelly,* which is twice the distance but a more gradual slope.

The bald area on the top is a wonderful place to look at the view while you have your picnic lunch. Monadnock is only 3,165 feet high but has gained its deserved reputation as a good hiking mountain because it is isolated, open on top, and much higher than nearby hills and smaller mountains like Little Monadnock to the southwest and Pack Monadnock to the northeast. In the winter you can also enjoy the network of cross-country ski trails in the park, which are marked according to their difficulty.

Dublin

When you have finished Monadnock continue north to Dublin, a beautiful New England town untouched by industry. Scotch-Irish settlers had arrived here by 1753, but the town was not incorporated until 1771. Mark Twain spent time in Dublin in the summer, finding it a peaceful place for writing.

FOR MORE INFORMATION

Jaffrey Chamber of Commerce, Jaffrey, NH 03452; (603) 532–4549

Monadnock Travel Council, Keene, NH 03431; (603) 355–8155

Peterborough Chamber of Commerce, Peterborough, NH 03458; (603) 924–7234

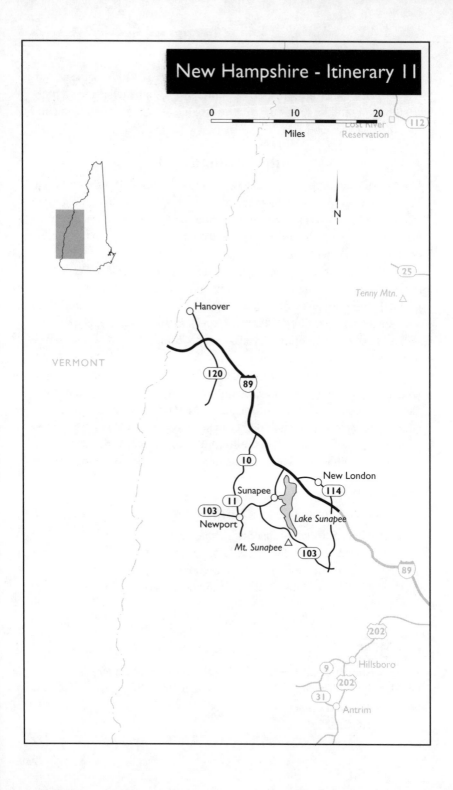

New Hampshire - Itinerary 11

0   10   20   Miles

Lost River
Reservation   112

25

Tenny Mtn.

Hanover

VERMONT

120   89

10

New London

Sunapee   114

103   11

Newport   Lake Sunapee

Mt. Sunapee   103

89

202

9   Hillsboro

202

31   Antrim

ITINERARY 11

Lake Sunapee Region • Hanover

Lake Sunapee Region

The conjunction of lake and mountain have made Lake Sunapee a favorite vacation area since the middle of the nineteenth century. You can take a cruise on the lake on one of the tour boats (603–763–4030) or ride up the mountains in a chairlift at *Mount Sunapee State Park* (603–763–2356) for a lovely view of the lake as a whole.

The *Mount Sunapee Ski Area* (603–763–2356) has long been a mecca for New Hampshire family skiers, with its 1,510 feet of vertical drop and 220 acres of skiable terrain served by nine lifts, now providing fifty-seven trails and slopes. More than half of them are rated for intermediate skiers, and some have stunning views of Lake Sunapee. Since it has been managed by Okemo Mountain in Vermont, Mount Sunapee has also drawn skiers from much farther afield. In recent years improvements have included two new quad chairlifts, a renovated lodge, improved snowmaking (with 97 percent coverage of trails) and grooming, and a new halfpipe for riders.

Cross-country skiers will enjoy the *Norsk Cross-Country Ski and Winter Sports Center* (603–526–4685) at the Lake Sunapee Country Club. A trail map will lead you around 70 kilometers of trails, forty-five of them tracked and thirty-two skate groomed. They also have 22 kilometers of backcountry trails for snowshoers.

If you're an aficionado of *covered bridges,* you will be delighted to know that there are eighteen in the Dartmouth-Lake Sunapee Region. Their locations are shown on New Hampshire highway maps with a symbol of a covered bridge. Look for them near the towns of Langdon, Cornish, Plainfield, Enfield, Lyme, Orford, Andover, Webster, Warner, Bradford, and Newport. Particularly notice the variations in truss work on these bridges, ranging from lattice to multiple kingpost designs. We especially like the name of one, "Blow Me Down," which is near Blow-Me-Down Hill in Cornish.

Hanover

From the Sunapee region Route 89 north will take you to Lebanon and Route 120 on to Hanover. It's the home of *Dartmouth College* (603–646–2100), founded in 1769 by the Reverend Eleazar Wheelock. His mission: to spread Christian education among the Indians. Dartmouth has had a distinguished undergraduate college for many generations and developed important medical, engineering, business, and computing programs in the twentieth century.

You can join a tour of the campus at the college information booth on the east side of the green during the summer. *Hopkins Center for the Performing Arts* offers concerts, an art gallery, and a theater. The *Baker Memorial Library* contains frescoes by Jose Clemente Orozco. Don't miss *Dartmouth Row,* a series of four classroom buildings dating from 1784. And when you're finished touring, stop for a meal in the *Hanover Inn* (800–443–7024 or 603–643–4300), which is right on campus.

FOR MORE INFORMATION

Lake Sunapee Business Association, Sunapee, NH 03782; (800) 258–3530 or (603) 763–2495; www.sunapee.vacations.com

Hanover Chamber of Commerce, Hanover, NH 03755; (603) 643–3115; www.hanoverchamber.org

New London Chamber of Commerce, New London, NH 02537; (603) 526–6575

Newport Chamber of Commerce, Newport, NH 03773; (603) 863–1510

ITINERARY 12

North Conway • Jackson
Pinkham Notch • Great Glen

You can make a circuit of the White Mountains in a variety of ways, stopping to ski or hike on various peaks according to the season. A good place to begin is *Conway,* where you can head west on the Kancamagus Highway to connect with Itinerary 14, head east on Route 302 to connect with Itinerary 21 in Maine, or head north on Route 16 into the Mount Washington valley.

There, on Itineraries 13 and 14, you will have access to some of the best hiking in the East on the network of trails through the Presidential Range; to great climbing in Huntington's Ravine; and to late spring skiing in the bowl of Tuckerman's Ravine, on the east face of Mount Washington. The latter is a New England spring ritual for slightly crazy die-hard skiers, but saner downhill skiers have a choice of six areas nearby—*Attitash Bear Peak, Wildcat Mountain, Mount Cranmore, Black Mountain, King Pine,* and *Bretton Woods.* Nordic skiers have extensive trail systems at *Jackson, Great Glen,* and *Bretton Woods,* and snowshoers can go almost anywhere.

For those who like to have four wheels under them, there are wonderful tours too, ranging from the hair-raising climb up the Mount Washington Toll Road to much easier drives through the mountains, including the classic *Kancamagus Highway* and major highways over Crawford Notch and Franconia Notch. No matter what the season, no one with mountain interests will be at a loss for activities in this region.

North Conway

From Conway, head north half a dozen miles on Routes 16 and 302 to North Conway. One of us remembers it as a quiet, classic New England town some forty or fifty years ago. Now it is a busy place all year round as the hub of the Mount Washington region, and it has become a center for outlet shopping, especially in outdoor wear and equipment. The bargain outlet prices have created a clutter of box-like stores along the highway, but other sections of town retain their more elegant New England ambience.

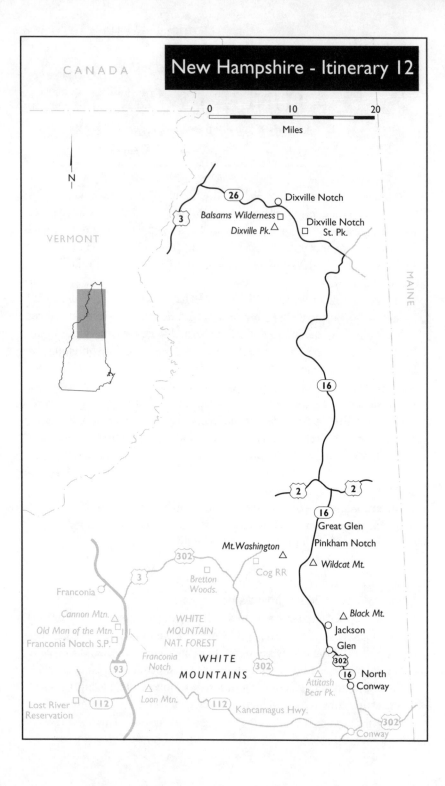

New Hampshire - Itinerary 12

CANADA

VERMONT

MAINE

0   10   20
Miles

N

26
3
Balsams Wilderness
Dixville Pk.
Dixville Notch
Dixville Notch
St. Pk.

16

2   2

16
Great Glen
Pinkham Notch
Wildcat Mt.

Mt. Washington
Cog RR
302
3
Bretton
Woods.

Franconia
Cannon Mtn.
Old Man of the Mtn.
Franconia Notch S.P.

Black Mt.
Jackson
Glen

WHITE
MOUNTAIN
NAT. FOREST

WHITE
MOUNTAINS

302
16
North
Conway

Franconia
Notch
93

Attitash
Bear Pk.

Lost River
Reservation
112

Loon Mtn.
112

Kancamagus Hwy.

302
Conway

The *Conway Scenic Railroad* (Norcross Circle, 603–356–5251) leaves from the century-old restored train station in town for two trips—"Valley Train" excursions to Conway and Bartlett, and a "Notch Train" trip through Crawford Notch. As seen from the highway far below, the latter runs on a roadbed that is indeed spectacular. There's also a railroad museum and a roundhouse on the station grounds.

To the west of town you'll find *Echo Lake State Park* (603–356–2672; follow the signs from the railroad station.) Come here for a swim or a picnic and see two dramatic rock formations—*White Horse Ledge* and *Cathedral Ledge.* You can drive to the top (some 700 feet) for a beautiful view of the valley.

At the eastern edge of town, *Cranmore Mountain Resort* (603–356–5544) has a vertical drop of 1,200 feet and nine lifts serving thirty-nine trails and glades on 192 acres of skiable terrain with 100 percent snowmaking coverage. When Austrian Hannes Schneider, often considered the father of American skiing, came to teach at Cranmore in 1939, his Arlberg technique became the standard of proficiency. One of us remembers first learning to ski there—as a matter of necessity, without the benefit of lessons—after being plopped at the top and told to head down slowly by companions before they pushed off.

At that time Cranmore was nicknamed "Kiddie Car Hill" because of its snowmobile lift, now long gone, but when we returned fifty years later the emphasis still remains on kids. As a family resort, Cranmore has always had excellent teaching and junior racing programs. Now, as one of eight Booth Creek resorts, it has added "snowtoys" for amusement—skibikes, skiboards, skifoxes, and snowscoots as well as an eight-lane snowtubing park. The sports center at the base of the mountain is unusually complete, with a pool, indoor tennis courts, workout equipment, a hot tub and an indoor climbing wall.

Jackson

Continue north on Route 16 through Glen to the right-hand turn-off into Jackson. There's a lovely covered bridge to go through as you enter this unspoiled New England village. Right in the center you will see cross-country trails branching out across the golf course during the winter.

The *Jackson Ski Touring Foundation* (800–927–6697 or 603–383–9355) also maintains an extensive network of more demanding cross-country trails in the surrounding mountainous terrain. This unique trail system, by far the largest in the East, and comprised of private and public land, was assembled in 1972, but the origin of the Jackson network goes back much farther, to 1888, making it the oldest Nordic trail system in the eastern U.S. Now this extensive and highly ranked trail network consists of 154 kilometers maintained by the Foundation and 32 more by the Appalachian Mountain Club: sixty trails connect seventeen inns and lodges, five pubs, ten eateries, and two alpine ski areas through three river valleys and 60 square miles of wilderness highlands. The Foundation grooms and double tracks 94 kilometers, as well as up to 94 kilometers for skating; provides information, a map, and a courtesy patrol; and sponsors events and programs. For those who want a relatively easy introduction to the beauties of this network, we recommend the *Ellis River Trail,* reached by branching off from the trail around the golf course.

Above Jackson on Route 16B, *Black Mountain* (800–475–4669 or 603–383–4490), one of the oldest alpine areas in the Mount Washington Valley, has served local skiers and visitors since 1935. With 1,100 feet of vertical drop, four lifts, forty trails with 143 acres of skiable terrain, and 98 percent snowmaking coverage, it maintains its identity as a classic and friendly New England ski area.

Jackson has a number of great places for a meal. Try the *Inn at Thorn Hill* (Thorn Hill Road, 603–383–4242); *Christmas Farm Inn* (Route 16B, 603–383–4313); *The Wentworth* (Route 16A, 603–383–9700); or *Yesterdays* (Jackson Village, 603–383–4457).

Pinkham Notch

From Jackson continue north on Route 16 to Pinkham Notch, where you will enter the heart of the terrain surrounding New England's highest and most extraordinary mountain. In the winter, the trails of *Wildcat Mountain Ski Area* (800–255–6439 or 603–466–3326) provide magnificent views of the summit and the ravines on the eastern face of Mount Washington. With a base at nearly 2,000 feet and a summit over 4,000 feet, Wildcat has a microclimate comparable to locations 900 miles north in Quebec, beyond the St. Lawrence River. In keeping with its wilderness setting, Wildcat does not allow trailside development of condos and chalets here.

Four lifts, including a detachable quad that gets you to the summit in six minutes, serve forty-four trails over 225 skiable acres. Although annual snowfall ranges from 175 to 250 inches, 90 percent of the terrain is also covered by snowmaking. There are several remarkable trails from the summit, including the 2 ¾-mile Polecat, a novice trail that allows beginners to ski the whole mountain, and an ungroomed trail for telemark experts leading down Wildcat Ridge to join the Jackson Touring Foundation network.

Tuckerman's Ravine at Pinkham Notch is the scene of a spring ritual for slightly crazy skiers and their only-a-bit-more-sane camp followers. The skiers carry skis and poles up the steep trail to the base of the ravine; the followers bring cameras, lunch, and the yen to watch. And what a show! A few skiers make it down the very steep bowl with style, the rest tumble down the hill—all to the cheers and boos of the crowd. The ravine, capped by an almost perfectly shaped bowl with a 50 degree headwall, has always lured extreme skiers, even before they were called that. In the 1930s an infamous race called the Inferno had a course starting in the snowfields below Mt. Washington's summit and plunging over the lip of the headwall into the ravine. It was reinvented in April 2001 as part of the *"Son of Inferno Pentathalon Event,"* sponsored by the *Friends of Tuckerman Ravine* (603–356–0131) to raise funds for the preservation of the ravine's historic uses.

At Pinkham Notch you'll see people getting ready to climb into Tuckerman's or one of the other ravines on the east face of the mountain. Of course, hiking is the best way to discover the beauty of the Presidential Range. The whole of the White Mountain National Forest is interlaced with well-marked hiking trails, lean-tos, and huts where you can get a bunk or a meal or both (reservations are a must in season; see below). This network allows you to travel light even on an extended hiking trip.

For information, guidebooks, and maps before you go, contact the Jackson Chamber of Commerce (800–866–3334) or the *Appalachian Mountain Club* (603–466–2727). The AMC also has a store in the camp at Pinkham Notch. Whether you're hiking the ravines or driving or riding the rails to the summit, dress warmly. Mount Washington records the highest wind velocities in the country, often well over 100 miles an hour during the winter. And the weather on top is changeable. The average temperature at any time of the year is below 30 degrees, and there's snow almost every month of the year. Always carry extra sweaters, jackets, and footwear in your backpack, as well as other emergency gear. Those who doubt the potential ferocity of a mountain only a little over 6,000 feet don't know this mountain, and they should read the list of those who didn't make it on the plaque at the summit.

Side Trip–Dixville Notch

If you have enjoyed Crawford Notch and Pinkham Notch in the Mount Washington region, you might want to take an extended side trip to even less populated country in the northern reaches of the state. From North Conway, take Route 16 north beyond Mount Washington, Gorham, and Berlin to Errol, then Route 26 west to Dixville Notch.

The Notch begins with a 10-percent grade just east of the Balsams Resort, as the road plunges downward. You can tell that glaciers left gaps as they advanced and receded. They approached from the back side of Mount Abeniki and cascaded down the front side, removing large boulders and leaving sheer cliffs. Glaciers continued plowing through the Notch, digging deeply and leaving steep walls. *Mount Abeniki* was named for the Indians who fished and hunted in the area. The *Coos Trail* was used by the Indians on their hunting expeditions; today it follows Route 26.

Back in the early 1800s Colonel Timothy Dix and his attorney and business partner, Daniel Webster, owned the land in the area. After Dix died in the War of 1812, Webster encouraged Betsy and John Whittemore, with their children, to move to Dixville Notch from Salisbury, New Hampshire. They were gracious hosts to any traveler going through the Notch. You'll see little caricatures of General John Adams Dix, Timothy Dix's son, around the Balsams Hotel.

The Balsams resort (800–255–0600 or 603–225–3400; also see Appendix) is the sort of place you can settle into and will really hate to leave at the end of your stay. How nice to have walking, hiking, golf, alpine and cross-country skiing, canoeing, rafting, mountain biking, and fishing available, along with a view that is magnificent enough to entice you to do nothing at all but enjoy it. As you approach during the winter, curvy roads through the mountains lead to views of the Balsams ski area from several angles. Suddenly *Lake Gloriette,* covered in snow, will come into view. The massive Balsams Hotel, with its roof peaks mirroring the mountains, stands across the lake. There's a special place at the hotel called the "Ballot Room," where Dixville Notch citizens are the "first in the nation" to vote for president, just after midnight on Election Day.

The Balsams Wilderness Alpine Ski Area (800–225–0600) has a vertical drop of 1,000 feet, three lifts, and thirteen trails on eighty-seven skiable acres with 80 percent snowmaking coverage. Novices will be comfortable on some of the easier trails from the top, as well as the separate beginners' slope, and intermediates will find most of the mountain to their liking. The trails have the classic New England character as they wind through the woods with small dips and curves that make you feel you are experiencing the natural contours of the mountain. In most ways this area reminds us of the medium-sized private mountains that flourished in the 1950s and 1960s—no lift lines, no crowds, no blaring music, and an elegant base lodge with good food.

The network of trails for cross-country skiing and snowshoeing in the Balsams Wilderness is far more ambitious, with 95 kilometers of trails winding through the 15,000 acres of wilderness that the resort owns. The trails are beautifully maintained, with 85 kilometers tracked both for striding and for skating and cover the range of all ability levels.

Dixville Notch State Park contains 137 acres of dramatic rocks and vistas—setting the anthropomorphic imaginations of local residents to work. From the road you can see a rock that looks like Martha Washington sitting in her rocker, wearing a night cap. Another rock resembles Daniel Webster looking over the landscape.

On the Three Brothers hiking trail, it takes about one hour to complete the 2-mile climb to the top. You will pass the Profile Cliff and Old King Cliff on the way up to Table Rock. On Huntington's Cascade walking trail you will pass the Whittemore grave site and reach Huntington's Cascade in another fifteen minutes. You can't miss the roaring sound of water rushing through the cut. The trail also leads to the southern end of the Three Brothers Trail.

If you'd like to spot a moose, try pausing on Route 26 between Cascade Brook Falls and Errol. Cars parked on the side of the road signal "moose watchers" at work. There is another good sighting place north of Pittsburg on Route 3, after the first Connecticut Lake, where there is a marsh . . . and moose.

From Colebrook (west of Dixville Notch), drive along Route 3 1 mile north of the Canadian border to the bottom of the hill. You're about to witness a "magnetic hill." Drive ¼ of a mile and turn around, head south on Route 3 toward the bottom of the hill and stop at the brown sign numbered UN, DEUX, TROIS. Stop opposite the sign and put your car in neutral. Then . . . your car will go uphill! Hard to believe but true.

Great Glen

From Pinkham Notch, continue north on Route 16 a few miles to Great Glen and the *Mount Washington Auto Road,* open from mid-May to late October. This is perhaps the most exciting way to reach the summit. If your car can take 8 miles of mountain driving with a lot of braking on the way down, then check it for gas and off you go! Be forewarned though: this is not a drive for the faint of heart, as a sign at the entrance suggests. The road, originally designed for carriages, is narrow and steep in places and runs close to the edge of large drops in some sections; it reminds us of the more exciting roads we have driven in the Rockies and the European Alps. You can also ride up in a van, leaving your mind free to enjoy the wonderful scenery.

During the winter, those interested in manageable cross-country skiing in this prime area surrounding Mount Washington will find it at the *Great Glen Trails Outdoor Center* (603–466–2333), where there are many routes for beginners and intermediates among the 40 kilometers of trails, half of them groomed or tracked. When conditions are right, more adventuresome skiers can ride up the Mount Washington Toll Road on a snow coach and take a run back down it. During the summer and fall months, this outdoor center offers many programs in hiking, biking, canoeing, kayaking, and fly-fishing.

FOR MORE INFORMATION

Jackson Chamber of Commerce, P.O. Box 304, Jackson, NH 03846; (800) 866–3334 or (603) 383–9356; www.jacksonnh.com

Mount Washington Valley Chamber of Commerce, P.O. Box 2300, North Conway, NH 03860; (800) 367–3364 or (603) 356–3171; www.mtwashingtonvalley.org

North Conway Welcome Center, Route 16, North Conway, NH 03860; (603) 356–3961

North Country Chamber of Commerce, Colebrook, NH 03576; (800) 698–8939 or (603) 237–8939

ITINERARY 13

Attitash Bear Peak • Bretton Woods
Mount Washington

Attitash Bear Peak

From North Conway, Route 302 will take you north and west around the other side of the big mountain that dominates the whole region. Half a dozen miles west of Glen, the junction where Routes 302 and 16 split, you'll reach New Hampshire's fastest growing ski resort, *Attitash Bear Peak* (Route 302, Bartlett, 603–374–2368), spread over two linked mountains. Originally created in 1965 as Attitash, a private membership resort, it later continued that tradition by limiting ticket sales to ensure that no one waited more than ten minutes in a lift line. The resort grew modestly until Les Otten bought it in 1994 and began an ambitious expansion plan to incorporate adjoining Bear Mountain into the area, with new lifts, trails, and facilities at both bases.

Now Attitash Bear Peak is the largest ski resort in New Hampshire, with a vertical drop of 1,750 feet on Attitash and 1,450 on Bear Peak. The complex is served by twelve lifts, including two high-speed quads; seventy trails and glades on the linked mountains provide 280 acres of skiable terrain, 97 percent of which is covered by snowmaking.

Large new structures at the base include the *Perfect Turn Discovery Center* at Attitash and the *Grand Summit Hotel and Conference Center* at Bear Peak. Attitash Bear Peak, now part of the American Skiing Company after the mergers of recent years, has also created innovations in tickets. It has a computerized system called "Smart Ticket," whereby skiers pay only for the rides they take. Each time a skier rides a lift, a certain number of points are deducted from the ticket, and the ticket is transferable. The "Smart Convertible" works on the same system but automatically becomes a day ticket if all the points are used up on the date of the purchase. There are a number of other ticket options, including a packet of seven that can be used at any American Skiing Company Resort.

Three miles west of Attitash Bear Peak, the *Bear Notch Ski Touring Center* (Route 302, Bartlett, 603–374–2277) has 70 kilometers of cross-

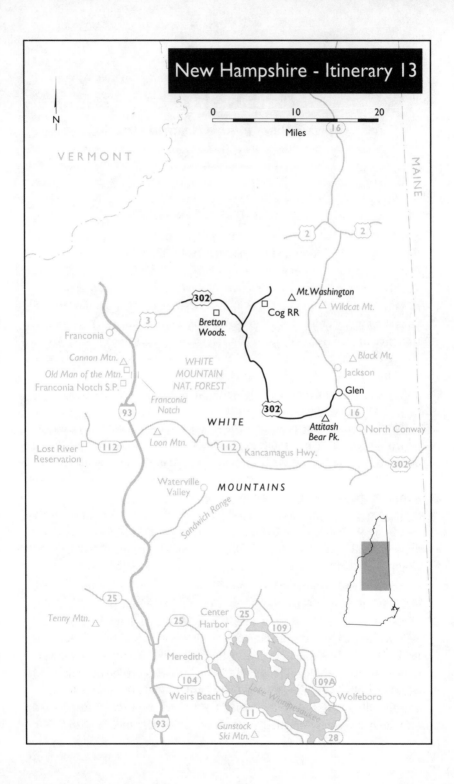

New Hampshire - Itinerary 13

0   10   20
Miles

VERMONT

MAINE

Mt. Washington

Wildcat Mt.

302

Cog RR

Bretton
Woods.

Franconia

WHITE
MOUNTAIN
NAT. FOREST

Black Mt.

Cannon Mtn.

Jackson

Old Man of the Mtn.

Glen

Franconia Notch S.P.

Franconia
Notch

302

93

WHITE

Attitash
Bear Pk.

16

North Conway

Lost River
Reservation

112

Loon Mtn.

112

Kancamagus Hwy.

302

Waterville
Valley

MOUNTAINS

Sandwich Range

25

Center
Harbor

25

109

Tenny Mtn.

25

Meredith

109A

104

Weirs Beach

Lake Winnipesaukee

Wolfeboro

11

93

Gunstock
Ski Mtn.

28

country trails, with 60 kilometers both tracked and groomed. Along with amenities such as a restaurant and trailside lodging, this area offers guided tours with staff naturalists.

Like other major New England ski areas, Attitash Bear Peak is increasing year-round resort activity. In summer, the alpine slide dives downward for a mile, and two water slides add to the fun. Other summer activities include guided horseback riding (603–374–2368), golfing, and hay rides, as well as the *White Mountain Jazz and Blues Festival* (603–356–5701) and an antiques show.

Bretton Woods

Farther west off Route 302, outlined against the big mountain, stands the massive grand old lady of the region—the *Mount Washington Hotel* at Bretton Woods (see Appendix), built by Pennsylvania Railroad tycoon Joseph Stickney and opened in 1902. It was the site of the watershed United Nations Monetary and Financial Conference in 1944, with representatives of forty-four nations in attendance. The foundations of the International Monetary Fund and World Bank were developed at the conference, as well as the gold standard, and the small parlor where the latter was established is still preserved intact in the hotel. This conference set the pattern for worldwide financial interdependence after World War II, creating the system we still live with. Through brass plates on guest-room doors indicating where the notable conferees slept, the hotel memorializes its role in that conference. On our last visit, we found ourselves sleeping in the room previously occupied by the most influential economic theorist of the twentieth century, John Maynard Keynes.

Through the vision and persistence of a group of New Hampshire owners who bought the aging hotel in 1991, it evaded the gradual deterioration and eventual abandonment that most such grand structures suffered. The new owners realized that the leisurely month- or summer-long holidays for the elite—a lifestyle from the late nineteenth into the early twentieth centuries—would never return. But the owners were able to envision new roles for an elegant historical hotel in an age of shorter getaway vacations for a much broader clientele. Recognizing that opportunities for outdoor recreation were abundant on the extensive grounds surrounding the hotel —golf, tennis, swimming, hiking, biking, riding—to draw guests for three seasons, the owners at first focused on the structure itself, getting the mechanical systems updated and restoring the elegance of the public spaces. They also provided modern amenities in the guest rooms. The hotel was never designed for year-round use, so the next step was to winterize it to take advantage of the ski season.

The winterized Mount Washington Hotel opened in November 1999 to usher in the new millennium. All of this made a lot of sense for a historic hotel with unbeatable views of Mount Washington, a renowned trail system for cross-country skiing, and a downhill ski area across the road.

On the hotel property, the *Bretton Woods Cross Country Ski Resort* is a major Nordic center with 100 kilometers of trails, 95 percent of them groomed and tracked. They begin on the golf course and reach up into the lower slopes below Mount Washington, with a network of forty-five trails spread through 1,770 acres of hotel property and 65 percent of them stretching into the White Mountain National Forest.

Across the highway, the *Bretton Woods Mountain Resort* (800–258–0330 or 603–278–3300) has always been one of the very best ski areas for novices and intermediates anywhere, and it is now expanding sideways onto adjoining peaks with some more difficult terrain. With a respectable 1,500 feet of vertical drop, it has eight lifts serving sixty-six trails on 345 skiable acres (including 130 acres of glades), 95 percent of which are covered by snowmaking (even though the area often gets more snow than other ski areas in the vicinity).

Built in 1972, the base lodge is attractive, and the slopes are lined with pines to look through as the snowflakes fall. Many of the trails afford superb views of Mount Washington, as does the *Top 'o Quad restaurant* on Mount Rosebrook, where you can get a gourmet lunch rather than the usual ski lodge fare.

When the Mount Washington Hotel bought the ski area in 1997, it began planning development to transform Bretton Woods into a major alpine resort. A few years back, a new 100-acre glade area opened as the first piece of West Mountain, on the right flank of the existing area. Now more advanced intermediate and a few expert runs have been created on West Mountain to broaden the appeal of the resort, and the big news is a continuing major expansion of alpine terrain eastward to Mount Stickney, scheduled to open in 2002 or 2003.

Mount Washington

Nearby, the historic *Mount Washington Cog Railway* (800–922–8825 or 603–278–5404), owned by some of the hotel partners, has its base station at Marshfield. You can leave the driving to them and have fun chugging up and down the mountain for an hour and a half each way in an 1868 railway. During the 3½ mile trip, the passenger cars are pushed uphill by a locomotive. If you go, watch for the very steep section known as Jacob's Ladder, where the grade is 37.4 percent; usually the grade is only 25 percent!

Mount Washington, at 6,288 feet, is the highest mountain in New England. It is also one of the coldest places in the United States, with much higher winds and lower temperatures than the surrounding region. It has what is considered an arctic climate, and the winds were once recorded at 231 miles per hour, in April 1934. The flora and fauna that grow there are seen only in arctic regions.

At the summit you will see radio and TV towers and the Sherman Adams Summit Building. If the weather is behaving, the rooftop deck provides nice views up to 50 miles in all directions. The Mount Washington Weather Observatory is perched up there, too, recording the most extreme weather conditions in the East and studying various problems of arctic survival and aeronautics.

For More Information

Mount Washington Valley Chamber of Commerce,
Box 2300, North Conway, NH 03860; (800) 367–3364 or (603) 356–3171

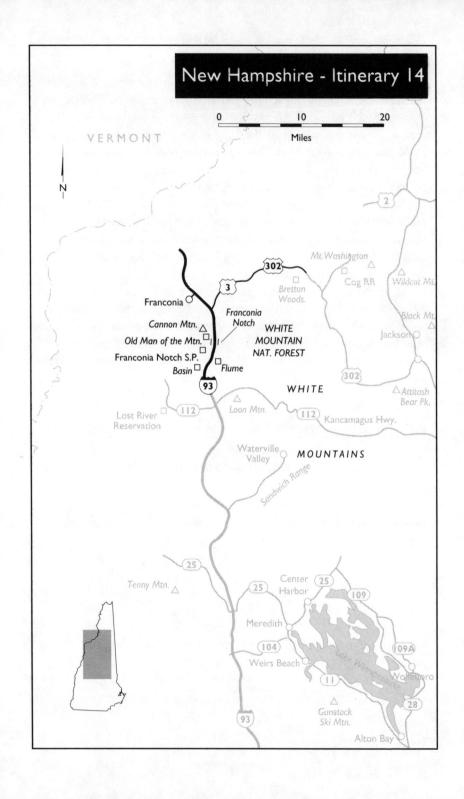

New Hampshire - Itinerary 14

0   10   20
Miles

VERMONT

N

3

302

Franconia

Mt. Washington

Cog R.R.

Wildcat Mt.

Bretton
Woods

Franconia
Notch

Cannon Mtn.

Old Man of the Mtn.

Franconia Notch S.P.

Basin   Flume

WHITE
MOUNTAIN
NAT. FOREST

Black Mt.

Jackson

302

93

WHITE

Attitash
Bear Pk.

Lost River
Reservation

112

Loon Mtn.

112   Kancamagus Hwy.

Waterville
Valley

MOUNTAINS

Sandwich Range

25

Tenny Mtn.

25

Center
Harbor

25

109

Meredith

104

Weirs Beach

109A

11

Lake Winnipesaukee

Wolfeboro

93

Gunstock
Ski Mtn.

28

Alton Bay

ITINERARY 14
Franconia • Cannon Mountain • Franconia Notch

Franconia

From Bretton Woods continue westward on Route 302 through **Bethlehem,** a resort center from earlier times now showing signs of revival, to the junction with I–93, then head south on the interstate to exit 38. Robert Frost spent summers and vacations from 1915 to 1920 in Franconia. His home—Robert Frost Place (603–823–5510)—has been restored, and mementos and photographs depict the poet's life here. The house is now an arts center, where a summer program of readings and lectures is conducted by a visiting poet-in-residence. To get here, take Route 116 south to Bickford Hill Road; turn right over the bridge, then left onto Ridge Road. For lunch or dinner in this region try the historic *Franconia Inn* (Easton Road, 603–823–5542), the *Sugar Hill Inn* (Route 117, 603–823–5621) or *Sunset Hill House* (Sunset Hill Road, 603–823–5522). (See Appendix for further details.)

Cannon Mountain

Rejoin I–93 heading south to exits 3 and 2 (numbered for the Franconia Notch Parkway section of I–93) to reach the *Cannon Mountain Aerial Tramway* (603–823–8800). Ride up to the summit, where gaps and notches give you a view right into the heart of the White Mountains. If you're there in the winter, try skiing *Cannon Mountain* (603–823–8800), advertised as "the mountain that'll burn your boots off!"

Indeed it will if you ski the expert trails, which really earn their ratings, but about half of the mountain is friendly to intermediates. In addition to the eighty-passenger aerial tramway—the first in North America—six other lifts serve forty-two trails with 163 skiable acres, 97 percent of them covered by snowmaking.

If you're a cross-country skier, try the *Franconia Notch State Park Trail System.* Begin from the parking lot at Echo Lake on Route 18 and enjoy over 5 miles of trails along old logging roads and old Route 3. Also, enjoy the trails of *Franconia Village Cross Country Ski Center* (800–473–5299) based in the Franconia Inn; it has 105 kilometers of trails, with 65 kilometers tracked. In nearby Sunset Hill, the *Sunset Hill House X-C Center* (603–823–5522) has 30 kilometers of trails.

The *New England Ski Museum* (800–639–4181 or 603–823–7177), located next to the aerial tramway base, opened in 1982 after five years of gathering artifacts. The displays change every year, and you will see a variety of vintage clothing. Some of us will remember when we wore laced boots and baggy pants, reindeer sweaters, shell tops, and mitts to protect our hands from icy rope tows!

Back then, wooden skis had cable bindings and poles sprouted large leather baskets. A collection of old skis ranges from homemade wooden models from the 1920s to the early post–World War II metal skis. Old and rare skis from around the world date back to 1900. When we visited the museum another permanent display on the Tenth Mountain Division caught our eye because we had seen similar information in Leadville, Colorado, near their training site.

Franconia Notch

The Franconia Notch Parkway takes you right through *Franconia Notch State Park* (603–823–8800), a lovely area surrounded by the White Mountains National Forest. Come to swim, hike, ski, camp—or simply enjoy the extraordinary natural beauty of the place. From north to south, you will come upon three noteworthy formations.

The first is the on the west side of the Parkway, above and beyond Profile Lake. Look up to see *Old Man of the Mountain* (he's sometimes called Great Stone Face) rising above the gorge. Plaques at the lake tell how the 40-foot-high profile was formed thousands of years ago. When this familiar landmark began to crumble through natural erosion, it was stabilized and is now watched over by a governor-appointed volunteer caretaker, now David Nielsen, Jr., after his father retired from the task. The extraordinary profile is the New Hampshire state emblem.

You next come to the *Basin,* also on the west side of the Parkway—a granite glacial pothole, 20 feet in diameter, which sits at the base of a waterfall. The information booth at Lafayette Place, located on the Franconia Notch Parkway, is the best place to stop for hiking information. Appalachian Mountain Club staff members are on hand to help you plan your own trail route.

Farther along, you will see the *Flume* on the east side of the Parkway. This narrow gorge has walls of granite rising 70 to 90 feet. The boardwalk along the 800-foot length of the gorge is lined with descriptions of its geological development and leads to the 40-foot *Avalanche Falls.*

For More Information

Franconia Notch Chamber of Commerce, Franconia, NH 03580; (800) 237–9007 or (603) 823–5661

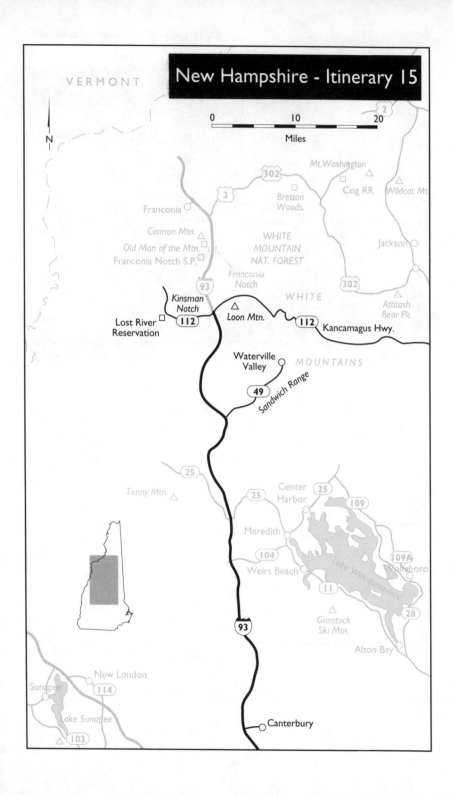

ITINERARY 15
Kinsman Notch • Loon Mountain • Waterville Valley

Kinsman Notch

From Franconia Notch drive south on I–93 to join this itinerary. To see another interesting geological formation, get off at exit 32 and drive west about 8 miles on Route 112 to **Kinsman Notch** and the **Lost River Reservation** (603–745–8031 or 603–745–2226). Lost River flows through a glacial gorge that is narrow, steep, and strangely shaped. Years ago boulders broke off and slid down into the gorge to form caverns. The **Giant Pothole** is a pear-shaped bowl, 28 feet across, worn smooth by swirling water. **Paradise Falls** was formed as the river flowed over two dikes and into a basin at the bottom. Also here: a natural history museum, an ecology trail, and a garden.

Loon Mountain

Return eastward through North Woodstock and Lincoln, where Route 112 becomes the Kancamagus Highway. Soon you will come to **Loon Mountain** (603–745–8111; lodging 800–227–4191), where you can ride a four-person gondola up 3,450 feet to see the view from the top. Climb up even higher to the observation tower for a panorama of the White Mountains.

For skiers, the vertical drop at Loon Mountain is 2,100 feet and the main exposure is north and northeast. Lifts include the gondola, a detachable quad, two triple chairlifts, three double chairlifts and a surface lift. Loon offers forty-four trails, two-thirds of them rated for intermediate skiers, with 98 percent snowmaking coverage. The area's 275 acres of ski terrain are spread over a series of peaks and ravines (with more sideways future expansion proposed), neatly linked at the top by a system of lifts and trails and at the bottom by a steam shuttle train.

Trails are named to reflect the mountain's logging history, of which original developer Sherman Adams was once a part. Loon has also been in the forefront of resorts in developing a wide range of winter activities, including other snowsports such as cross-country skiing, snowshoeing, night tubing, and skating, as well as a children's theater and a wildlife theater.

During the winter, Loon follows the policy of limiting the sale of lift tickets to keep lines to a minimum. Summer activities include hiking, horseback riding, biking, nature walks, croquet, archery, rollerblading, and tennis, as well as attending lectures, concerts, and the theater.

Stop for a meal in *Seasons on Loon* or *Black Diamond Bar and Grill* in The Mountain Club on Loon right on the slope (603–745–2244). Or drive into town and wander through the shops and restaurants in the *Millfront Marketplace*. Nearby, in North Woodstock, the *Woodstock Inn* (603–745–3951) is open for all meals. One of their rooms is housed in the Woodstock Station, which was moved from the tracks and placed adjacent to the inn.

Waterville Valley

Drive south on I–93 and east on Route 49 to reach another well-established New Hampshire destination, Waterville Valley (603–236–8311; lodging 800–468–2553). This year-round resort offers skiing, ice skating, and snowboarding in the winter and tennis, riding, golf, horseback riding, hiking, and swimming in the summer. It is located in a bowl surrounded by 4,000-foot mountains. In the winter there is a special appeal for the "I Don't Ski" population—a spa program as well as the complete facilities of the White Mountain Athletic Club.

Waterville Valley has always been full of upscale amenities, too. You can have an elegant five-course dinner at the mountaintop *Schwendi Hutte* on certain winter evenings, or take a gourmet lunch tour from the Nordic Center.

The vertical drop is 2,020 feet on Mount Tecumseh. There are eleven lifts, including two high-speed quads, serving fifty-two trails on 225 acres of skiable terrain, much of it rated for intermediates. Waterville Valley has been limiting admission on busy weekends to keep skiers from being overwhelmed by long lift lines. Since Waterville was purchased by Booth Ski Holdings in 1996, investment has been poured into developing the mountain and its facilities, including new lifts, an expanded base lodge, a new restaurant, a kids terrain park, and improved snowmaking on 100 percent of the mountain.

If you or your spouse have reached the age of fifty-five, you can join the "Silver Streaks Club" on Monday through Thursday for special benefits: reduced lift, lodging, learn-to-ski, and cross-country skiing prices, reserved parking, races, clinics, and more. Some people come every week for fun, parties, and skiing with new friends. In 1998, a Silver Streak member, Nate Grifkin, won the national Master's giant slalom championship and placed second in the downhill at the age of 76.

Side Trip–Kancamagus Highway

From Lincoln, head east past Loon Mountain on Route 112, known in this section as the *Kancamagus Highway,* one of the most scenic drives in the northeast. The Kancamagus Highway stretches from the Pemigewasset River at Lincoln to the Saco River at Conway, New Hampshire. You won't be bored as you round each hairpin turn of this 34-mile drive. There are gorges, falls, and overlooks with superb mountain views all along this wilderness highway.

Kancamagus, the "fearless one," was the grandson of Passaconaway, chief of the Algonquin Indians, and became chief himself in 1684. Although he tried to encourage harmony between the Indians and the white men, war broke out and his tribe moved away. Chocorua was another brave Indian, probably a chief of the Ossipee tribe, who lived in the area about 1760. Legends suggest that he died on the summit of Mount Chocorua, south of the Kancamagus Highway.

Don't miss stopping to see *Sabbaday Falls,* a five-minute walk each way. It is actually a series of falls tumbling over ledges, into potholes, and finally through a flume. The Saco Ranger District (603–447–5448), located at beginning of Route 112 in Conway, offers information on White Mountain National Forest.

One hundred kilometers of cross-country trails are also available, including a challenging 6-kilometer race training course. There are also music festivals and concerts.

Stop for lunch in the *T-Bar* (603–236–8311). The Town Square offers a variety of restaurants, the *Valley Inn and Tavern* (603–236–8336).

Side Trip–Canterbury

Follow I-93 south to exit 18, then drive east through Canterbury Center and follow signs for *Canterbury Shaker Village* (603–783–9511). Here you will find twenty-four Shaker buildings that now form a living-history museum. The village was founded in the 1780s as the sixth of nineteen U.S. Shaker communities. Shaker furniture includes simple but aesthetically remarkable beds, chairs, chests, work tables, benches, baskets, and more. The Shakers devoted their "hands to work, hearts to God."

You can watch craftsmen weaving, spinning, printing, making brooms and baskets, woodworking, and tinsmithing. You may also sign up in advance for workshops and learn how to make brooms, herbal wreaths, and baskets yourself, or you might engage in woodworking or weaving projects. When you're hungry, try the *Creamery Restaurant* on the grounds, which serves Shaker-inspired meals.

For More Information

Lincoln/Woodstock Chamber of Commerce, Lincoln, NH 02351; (603) 745–6621; reservations (800) 227–4191; www.linwoodcc.org

Maine

The Pine Tree State

Our images of Maine are mostly maritime—waves crashing on rocky promontories, crisp mornings licked by wisps of fog, huge jumbled shoreline rock formations. This bedrock of the state was formed during the Precambrian era, which produced weathered formations of sandstone and limestone. Other sections with rich beds of fossils date from the Paleozoic era.

During the Ice Age the weight of the ice cap caused the land to sink below sea level. Water flooded into long valleys, creating fjords and coves, and leaving clay as much as 75 miles away from the modern shoreline. Some clay deposits, exposed by running streams and excavations, are now 500 feet above sea level. As the glacier dissolved, mountains that were near the shore became islands, and those that were farther inland became headlands jutting into the sea, creating a drowned coastline that's one of the most fascinating anywhere in the world.

The first inhabitants of Maine were roving hunters, Native American descendants of Asian immigrants who crossed the land bridge when the Bering Strait was dry. Their graves, found in more than fifty tribal cemeteries, contain red ochre (powdered hematite), which gave them the name "Red Paint People." Heavy stone tools were found in the same graves. Later Native peoples called themselves Wabanackis, which means "easterners" or "dawnlanders," and their language was that of the Algonquin tribes. Today, there are two tribes left: the Passamaquoddies and the Penobscots.

The first foreigners to arrive in Maine were probably the Vikings, who had occupied islands and coastal towns in the North Sea from the late eighth to the late twelfth centuries, then pushed west to colonize first Iceland and Greenland, followed by Newfoundland and Nova Scotia. Leif Erikson sailed to Newfoundland in 1003 and continued past Maine to Cape Cod. Several years later his brother Thorvald landed in Maine, probably at Somes Sound, a fjord cutting into Mount Desert Island, where he was killed by Indians.

In 1496 John Cabot and his sons Lewis, Sebastian, and Sancius received permission from King Henry VII of England to look for and occupy new lands. Between 1497 and 1499 they made a number of voyages along the Maine coast—voyages that formed the basis of England's claim to Maine and other parts of North America.

In 1542 Giovanni da Verrazano, an Italian explorer serving under the French flag, also reached Maine, but he did nothing to establish a settlement. And a year later, Esteban Gomez, a Spanish explorer, left this area, too, when he did not find the gold he was looking for. Not until the seventeenth century did European explorers fully realize the treasure that was here in fish, fur, and timber.

In 1614 Captain John Smith arrived in Maine and named the coastline from Nova Scotia to Cape Cod "New England." The origin of the state's name isn't clear: Some believe the name was a tribute to Queen Henrietta Marie, because she ruled the French provinces of Meyne or Maine; others believe that the name was derived from "mainland." But to sailors of later eras the question was moot because Maine was always "Down East." Why? You could get there easily from other parts of New England by running downwind on the prevailing southwesterly winds. Getting back was another matter, usually requiring a long and hard beat to windward.

The Maine Coast

These itineraries will take you "down east" along the coast of Maine, all the way from the New Hampshire border to Mount Desert Island. They explore unusually attractive coastal regions dear to the hearts of residents and frequently visited by travelers from all over the world. The southern section of this shore begins at Kittery with salt marshes and fine sand beaches, interspersed with rocky promontories as you move northeastward. Then the relatively straight coast is interrupted by Casco Bay, filled with many islands and locked between Portland harbor to the south and the first of many peninsulas to the north.

The mid-coast section, northeast of Casco Bay, resembles Norwegian fjords with a network of fingers of the sea stretching far inland in drowned river valleys. Many years ago, saltwater farms provided marsh grass for thatch and fodder, and farmers sometimes rowed from field to field. This intricate maze of peninsulas comes to a halt at Rockport, where the coast's largest inlet begins. Penobscot Bay is lined with classic Maine seaport towns from Camden to Castine and is the base for many fishermen, and for the fleet of Maine cruise schooners and innumerable

pleasure boats. In Penobscot's center three large islands—Vinalhaven, North Haven, and Islesboro—are filled with vacation homes, and two more, Deer Isle and Isle au Haut, protect its eastern fringes from exposure to the full Atlantic swell.

Farther eastward Mount Desert is the coast's largest and most dramatic island, with Cadillac Mountain rising 1,530 feet above sea level. In the late nineteenth century, the island became famous as home to Bar Harbor, the principal resort for affluent New Englanders who eschewed the pretentiousness of Newport mansions but nevertheless built substantial summer homes along the shore. In the twentieth century, the focus has shifted to Acadia National Park, one of the East's most popular sites for hiking, cycling, boating, or just sitting along the coast in magnificent natural surroundings.

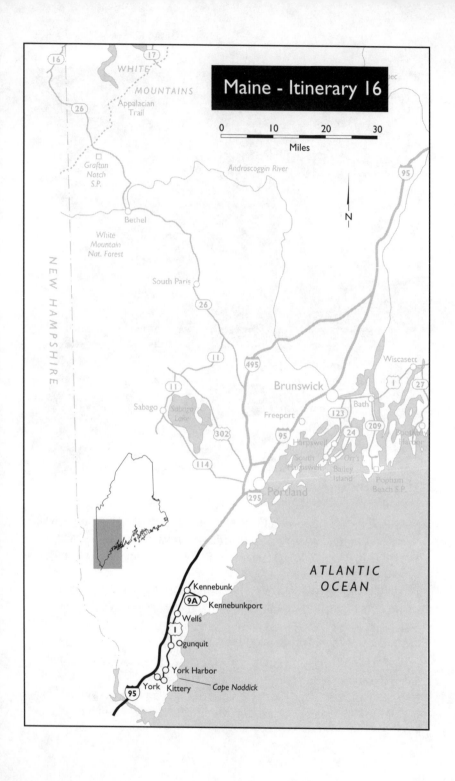

Maine - Itinerary 16

WHITE MOUNTAINS
Appalacian Trail
Graftan Notch S.P.
Androscoggin River

NEW HAMPSHIRE

Bethel

White Mountain Nat. Forest

South Paris

Wiscasett

Brunswick

Sabago
Sabago Lake

Freeport

Bath

Harpswell

South Harpswell

Orr's Island

Bailey Island

Popham Beach S.P.

Portland

ATLANTIC OCEAN

Kennebunk

Kennebunkport

Wells

Ogunquit

York Harbor

York   Kittery   Cape Naddick

ITINERARY 16

Kittery • York • York Harbor • Cape Neddick
Ogunquit • Wells • Kennebunk • Kennebunkport

From Portsmouth, New Hampshire, take I–95 or Route 1 across the Piscataqua River into Kittery.

Kittery

Kittery, incorporated in 1647, is the state's oldest town and has long depended on shipbuilding as its major industry. The *Ranger,* which sailed to France under the command of John Paul Jones to announce Burgoyne's surrender, was built here. The *John Paul Jones Marker* is located at the end of the park on Route 1 at the intersection of Government Street.

Kittery Historical and Naval Museum (Rogers Road, 207–439–3080) features a 13-foot model of the *Ranger,* as well as other models of eighteenth, nineteenth, and twentieth-century naval vessels. Exhibits portray the life of those who lived on the Piscataqua River and the story of the development of shipbuilding in Kittery.

Drive along the coastal road toward Kittery Point past several homes dating back to 1690 (not open to the public): the *Fernald House* on Williams Avenue, the *Whipple Garrison House* on Whipple Road, and *Willowbank,* the home of the artist John P. Benson, also on Whipple Road. Look to the right to see the *Naval Shipyard* located on two islands in the Piscataqua River. Although the shipyard is not open for public visits, you can see exhibits on its work at the Kittery Museum.

Kittery Point is the oldest part of town. The *Lady Pepperell House* on Pepperell Road, a striking white Georgian mansion, is a private residence. There is an interesting graveyard beyond the house, overlooking the harbor. Look there for Robert Browning's epitaph for the husband of poet Celia Thaxter carved on an irregular stone.

The grave of unknown sailors who died when the *Hattie Eaton* ran aground on Garrish Island is also there. Many ships foundered along the treacherous coastline between Kittery Point, Boon Island, and Cape Neddick. Read *Boon Island* by Kenneth Roberts to set your spine tingling. Names on other old stones are still well known in the area.

Farther up the road you come to ***Fort McClary State Historic Site*** (Route 103, 207–384–5160). The fort provided protection against the French and Indians as well as pirates. It was named Fort William after Sir William Pepperell, a Kittery native knighted by the British for his leadership of the Louisbourg expedition in 1745, then renamed during the Revolution, when commemoration of a victory of combined British and colonial forces over the French seemed inappropriate.

The hexagonal blockhouse, brick magazine, and barracks were built some years later. Photographers may want to stand below the blockhouse and look up for an unusual shot. Sit back and enjoy the view of the outer harbor—hundreds of sailboats bobbing on moorings, fishing boats going in and out, and a maze of lobster pots everywhere.

Fort Foster sits as a sentinel for Portsmouth Harbor. Built in 1872, the bunkers now lie idle among the ducks and other shore birds that pass through. The park contains picnic facilities, beaches, and a fishing pier. There are two beaches there, one 200 feet long and one 400 feet. Both are clean and sandy and sprinkled with rocks. ***Sea Point Beach,*** off Route 103 on Cutts Island Road, is also sandy with some rocks.

York

York, north of Kittery on Route 1A, contains a National Historic District, and many of the seventeenth- and eighteenth-century homes in the village are open. Turn off Route 1A at Lindsay Road and park your car in the lot. The ***Old York Historical Society*** (207–363–4974) maintains a living history village of seven historic buildings in York. ***Jefferds' Tavern,*** on Lindsay Road, is the place to get information. Visitor tours begin in this building, a mid-eighteenth-century saltbox tavern that was built in Wells and moved to its present location in the 1940s. Interpreters engage in a variety of craft and living history demonstrations here.

Take a walk through the ***Old Burying Ground.*** Mary Nason's grave is covered with a giant stone slab. According to legend she was a witch and the slab was put there to keep her soul in the grave. The truth is almost as good: Her heartbroken husband, a wealthy man, placed the stone there to keep the village pigs from grazing on her grave.

At the other end of the graveyard you come to the ***Emerson-Wilcox House.*** The house was built in 1740 on church land, then leased for 999 years. It was once a tailor shop, tavern, and general store, and then a post office. Today its rooms are furnished in a series of different period styles.

One of them boasts a local treasure, the Mary Bulman bed hangings—the only complete set of eighteenth-century American crewelwork hangings in the U.S.

Across the street you'll find the *Old Gaol Museum.* It was a king's prison from 1719 through the Revolution and continued to be used as a jail until 1860. You can walk through the jailer's quarters, the cells, and the dungeon—a special treat for children.

From the Old Gaol cross York Street (Route 1) to the *First Parish Congregational Church,* on the green. The Reverend Samuel Moody laid the cornerstone in 1747. The Reverend Joseph Moody, his son, was the subject of one of Hawthorne's short stories, "The Minister's Black Veil." Moody accidentally killed a friend while they were out hunting and felt so guilty that he wore a handkerchief over his face for the rest of his life.

Head back across York Street to the other end of Lindsay Road, near the parking lot, to see the *Old Schoolhouse,* which was built in 1745. From here you can drive or walk (it's about a mile) down Lindsay Road to the river. The John Hancock Warehouse (Hancock was one of the owners) houses an exhibit about life and industry on the York River. This eighteenth-century commercial building—the only surviving one in the area—is set up as a period warehouse. Outside you can enjoy a picnic lunch by the water.

The Elizabeth Perkins House sits beside the river at Sewall's Bridge. Perkins, who died in the 1950s, and her mother were largely responsible for the preservation work in the village. The eighteenth-century Colonial house, once the Perkins's summer home, is filled with their marvelous collection of furnishings from all over the world.

York Harbor

York Harbor's waterfront is bustling. Don't miss *Cliff Walk,* which begins along the boardwalk at the ocean end of Harbor Beach Road and ends on a rocky beach near Cow Beach Point. Along the way you'll get wonderful views of the coastline (look for Nubble Light to the north), see lovely homes, and hear the sounds of waves crashing over the rocks.

Cape Neddick

Follow Route 1A to Nubble Road, leading to the tip of Cape Neddick. Next to *Nubble Light* is the six-bedroom Victorian lightkeeper's house. Captain Bartholomew Gosnold landed here in 1602, and named the point

Savage Rock because of an encounter he had with the Indians on shore. The lighthouse was built in 1879 after the rock had claimed several ships.

From the point you can see **Boon Island Lighthouse,** 6½ miles southeast of the cape. Celia Thaxter describes the lonely life of the lightkeeper and his family in *The Watch of Boon Island.*

Ogunquit

Continue on Route 1A up the coast to Ogunquit. The 2½-mile-long beach here is one of the finest in New England—but the water is cold! The mile-long **Marginal Way,** a path along the ocean, begins at SparHawk Motel and ends at Shore Road in Perkins Cove. This is an easy, paved walk between the ocean and shorefront homes on an interesting section of rocky coast. There are even benches along the way for restful contemplation of the view. This walk is somewhat unusual along New England coastlines, originally donated by a longtime resident and repaired by donations of many others after a nor'easter tore it apart. The Marginal Way reminds us of similar walks in Europe—where general access to seafront is taken for granted rather than regarded as a special privilege—as well as the Cliff Walk in Newport, Rhode Island.

After the walk, you can stop to browse in one of the galleries in **Perkins Cove.** The cove is filled with artists and craftspeople, lobstermen and fishing boats, and lots of good restaurants. Look for the double-leaf-draw footbridge, the only one in Maine, which is raised for every boat that sounds a horn.

If you're a fan of lobster, stop for a meal at **Barnacle Billy's** in Perkins Cove (800–866–5575 or 207–646–5575), where the menu hasn't changed for three decades. The 3½-ounce lobster roll is just as delicious now as it was originally. You can sit outdoors on the sundeck or inside if you wish. Don't be put off by the valet parking—it's necessary to squeeze in as many cars as possible. There's another Barnacle Billy's next door.

The **Ogunquit Playhouse** (Route 1, 207–646–5511) has been delighting people since the 1930s. The theater offers well-known musicals and plays.

Wells

Wells is about 5 miles north of Ogunquit, on Route 1. The **Wells Auto Museum** (Route 1, 207–646–9064) is fun for the whole family. You'll find collections of cars, bicycles, motorcycles, and even license plates and nickelodeons.

The **Rachel Carson National Wildlife Refuge** (Route 9, 207–646–9226) is a lovely stop for communing with nature. The white-pine forest stands next to a salt marsh, where you can spot herons, kingfishers, and egrets. A 1-mile, self-guided, accessible trail leads through the woods and into the marsh on a circular route. You can walk part of the way on a board-walk over the marsh.

Adjacent to the refuge is a nature center called the **Wells National Estuarine Research Reserve** (207–646–1555) with headquarters at Laudholm Farm, a well-preserved nineteenth-century saltwater farm. This estuarine environment offers special plants, fish, and wildlife for study. It is a natural field laboratory for research and education as well as a place for people to observe nature where a river meets the sea.

Kennebunk

Continue up the coast along Route 1 to Kennebunk. Main Street boasts an interesting church and the *Brick Store Museum* (117 Main Street, 207–985–4802), where you'll find a collection of early American pewter, maritime exhibits, old wedding gowns, and antique fire engines. Ask for a map of the other historic homes in town (most aren't open to the public).

There's a legend about one of these homes—the *Wedding Cake House.* The sea captain who built the house created the elaborate trimming for his disappointed bride; they had married so quickly that there wasn't time to bake a wedding cake.

Kennebunkport

Take Route 9A from Kennebunk to Kennebunkport, where you'll find the oldest commercial building in the area. It began as Perkins' West India Goods, then became a boardinghouse, a post office, a harness shop, a fish market, an artist's studio, and today it's a bookshop called *Book Port* (800–382–2710 or 207–967–3815). It's in Dock Square, a good spot for watching the Kennebunkport world go by.

The *Kennebunkport Historical Society* (North End, 207–967–2751) features exotic treasures brought back by sea captains, exhibits about local shipwrecks, and other memorabilia. Many of the towns along the New England coast had their own ropewalks—long platforms with a spindled wheel at either end. The ropemakers would walk between the wheels, spinning flax (or later hemp) as they went. Thomas Goodwin built a ropewalk on Ocean Avenue, Kennebunkport, in 1806. (It's now a yacht club.) The platform here was 600 feet long. Because each wheel had six spindles, six men would have worked spinning flax here.

Stop at the *Seashore Trolley Museum* (Log Cabin Road, 207–967–2800) for a ride on an old-fashioned trolley. Also here you'll see a slide show, exhibits from horsecars to steamliners, and craftsmen at work restoring the collection.

One of the most relaxing things to do is to take a shore walk. *Kennebunk Beach* walk encompasses a series of beaches along Beach Avenue from Gooch's Beach past Lord's Point. It's a great place to bring a picnic supper and watch the sunset angling over the coastline. The distance from Gooch's Beach to Lord's Point is about 1½ miles one way, so it isn't arduous.

Goose Rocks Beach, east of Kennebunkport, is famous for its fine white sand. Goose Rocks, a mecca for migrating birds, is visible offshore at low tide. You may spot a piping plover in the beach grass on the dunes. Goose Rocks Beach is about 3 miles long one way from end to end.

Parson's Way Walk, from the center of Kennebunkport through Henry Parson's Park, has several natural features along the way: *Spouting Rock* and *Blowing Cave.* Both make noises and spray as air is compressed during high tides. You can see former President Bush's summer home at *Walker's Point* from this shore. The distance along Parson's Way is 4.8 miles round-trip, beginning at Dock Square.

Don't leave town without stopping for lunch or supper at one of the many restaurants. Our favorites: *The Breakwater* (207–967–3118) on Ocean Avenue; *The White Barn Inn* (207–967–2321) on Beach Street; *Arundel Wharf* (207–967–3444) on the waterfront; and *Seascapes* in nearby Cape Porpoise (207–967–8500).

For More Information

Gateway to Maine Chamber of Commerce, 306 US Route 1, P.O. Box 526, Kittery, ME 03904; (800) 639–9645 or (207) 439–7545. www.gatewaytomaine.org

Kennebunk–Kennebunkport Chamber of Commerce, 17 Western Avenue, P.O. Box 740, Kennebunk, ME 04043; (207) 967–0587; www.kkcc.maine.org

Ogunquit Chamber of Commerce, Route 1 South, P.O. Box 2289, Ogunquit, ME 03907; (207) 646–2939; www.ogunquit.org

Wells Chamber of Commerce, 136 Post Road, Route 1, P.O. Box 356, Wells, ME 04090; (207) 646–2451; www.wellschamber.org

York Chamber of Commerce, 571 U.S. Route 1, York, ME 03909; (800) 639–2442 or (207) 363–4422; www.yorkme.org

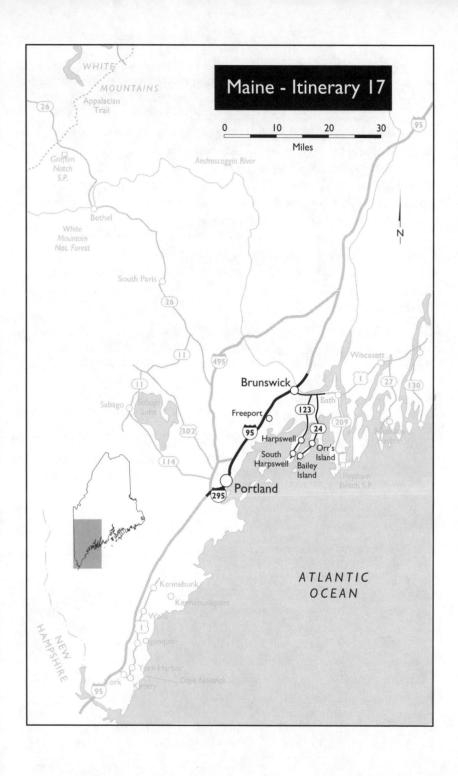

WHITE
MOUNTAINS
Appalacian
Trail

26

Grafton
Notch
S.P.

Androscoggin River

0   10   20   30
Miles

95

Bethel

White
Mountain
Nat. Forest

South Paris

26

N

11

495

Wiscasett

11

1   27   130

Sabago   Sabago
Lake

Brunswick

Bath

Freeport

123

302

95   Harpswell

209

114   South
Harpswell   24   Orr's
Island

Bailey
Island   Popham
Beach S.P.

295   Portland

ATLANTIC
OCEAN

Kennebunk

Kennebunkport

Wells

1

Ogunquit

NEW
HAMPSHIRE

York Harbor

Cape Nodick

York

Kittery

95

ITINERARY 17

Portland • Freeport • Brunswick
The Harpswells • Orr's Island/Bailey Island

Portland

From Kennebunkport take Route 9A to I–95, then head north to Portland. Stop at the **Convention and Visitor's Bureau** (305 Commercial Street, 207–772–5800) for information about self-guided walking tours. In addition, **Greater Portland Landmarks** (165 State Street, 207–774–5561) offers guided walking tours of the city from July to September. The service also offers a series of special summer tours, including some to Casco Bay islands. **Mainely Tours** runs bus tours of Portland that include the Old Port district and Portland Head Light. Tours depart from the visitor's bureau from May to October. Call (207) 774–0808 for more information.

Next head for the waterfront and the **Old Port Exchange.** This area, devastated by the Great Fire of 1866, was restored in the 1970s. It's filled with shops, restaurants, pubs, and recreational facilities. Along the wharves you'll see fish-processing plants and warehouses. And the harbor is busy with ferries and boats heading out to Nova Scotia and Casco Bay. You can wander around endlessly, watching the waterfront activity and savoring the smell of the sea.

There are two good restaurants nearby: **Pepperclub,** 78 Middle Street (207–772–0531), and **F. Parker Reidy's** (207–773–4731) on Exchange Street. Or bring a picnic and enjoy the fine view over the bay on the **Eastern Promenade,** a good spot for watching Fourth of July fireworks. (Across the harbor, **Falmouth Foreside** offers a fine anchorage for visiting yachts.)

The first brick house to be constructed in Portland was the **Wadsworth-Longfellow House** (487 Congress Street, 207–879–0427). It was built in 1785 by Henry Wadsworth Longfellow's grandfather, General Peleg Wadsworth. The house contains Wadsworth and Longfellow family furnishings, including crocheted tablecloths and needlework samplers. Other period pieces are from the collection of the Maine Historical Society. The Longfellows and the Wadsworths were both descended from Pilgrims who came on the *Mayflower.* Henry Wadsworth Longfellow lived in the house as a child with his seven brothers and sisters, parents, and an aunt. The *Maine Historical Society Summer Gallery* (207–774–1822) is next door to the house. Visitors are invited to stroll in the garden behind the house.

George Tate, who was responsible for selecting and blazing mast trees with the "King's Arrow," built the *Tate House* (1270 Westbrook, 207–774–9781) in 1755. His Georgian house is unusual with its indented clerestory gambrel roof, which is a recessed windowed section above the second story designed to let in light. Inside, the house is furnished with pieces that depict the lifestyle of a wealthy official during the eighteenth century.

The hall contains a dogleg stairway and the original cove ceiling. Collections include pottery, porcelain, silver, and textiles; pewter and iron kitchen utensils are also on display. Family letters and memorabilia give insight into the Tate family. Outside, the raised-bed herb garden contains typical eighteenth-century plants.

The *Victoria Mansion* (109 Danforth Street, 207–772–4841) is also called the *Morse-Libby House.* This brownstone, built in the Italian villa style, is hard to miss with its soaring square tower. Inside, you will see stained-glass windows, etched glass, frescoes, and carved woodwork. The furniture is the original Morse collection.

For a view of the White Mountains, Casco Bay, and the city of Portland, head for the *Portland Observatory* (138 Congress Street, 207–774–5561), where you can climb 102 steps for the view. The observatory once served as a signal tower; flags were raised when vessels were spotted approaching the harbor.

Portland has a number of notable galleries and museums. The *Portland Museum of Art,* designed by I. M. Pei (Seven Congress Square, 207–775–6148), houses many nineteenth- and twentieth-century works, including some by Andrew Wyeth, Winslow Homer, and Marsden Hartley. The *Stein Glass Gallery* (195 Middle Street, 207–772–9072) offers the largest collection of work by New England glass artists in the United States. And the *Osher Map Library* (207–780–4850) on the campus of the *University of Southern Maine* has one of the best collections of maps, atlases, city plans and views in the Northeast.

Freeport

From Portland follow I–95 north to Freeport for a shopping spree at *L. L. Bean* (800–341–4341 or 207–865–4761). Here is everything you could pos-

sibly want for camping, canoeing, climbing, fishing, hiking, hunting, kayaking, skiing, and snowshoeing. Even if you're not an outdoors person, you'll love poking around the clothing and book sections of this fabulous place.

As all Yankees know, L. L. Bean is not so much a store as a Maine institution, and one open twenty-four hours a day, 365 days a year at that. Stopping at the big store at 95 Main Street is a ritual for outdoor folks passing through. We stock up on traditional Bean items like chamois shirts or hiking jackets, and one of us always makes a long pause at the racks of Old Town canoes and kayaks, another Maine standby. We've had our famous Bean boots for years, and they can even be renovated to avoid giving up that comfortable broken-in feel. There's also a factory store on Depot Street where you can find Bean bargains.

The store sponsors a wide range of **Outdoor Discovery Schools** in fly-fishing, paddling, cycling, shooting, and other outdoor skills, as well as winter activities. These can include map and compass reading, bush-whacking in the mountains, a wildlife workshop on Swan Island, back-packing in Baxter State Park, and lessons in outdoor photography. You can choose to head off on a weeklong expedition or simply take a two-hour class while you're in town. Call (800) 341–4341, ext. 6666 for information and schedules.

More than one hundred new outlet stores, shops, and restaurants have opened in Freeport during the past decade. "Free" indeed! After a sprint of shopping you may be ready for a meal. Try *Harraseeket Inn (*162 Main Street, 207–865–9377) for a dinner in the main dining room or a lighter meal in the Broad Arrow Tavern. On the waterfront, *Harraseeket Lunch & Lobster Company* (Main Street, 207–865–4888) offers fresh seafood with a view.

Brunswick

Continue on I–95 to Brunswick, the home of *Bowdoin College.* On cam-pus stop to see paintings by Stuart, Copley, Homer, and Eakins in the *Museum of Art* (207–725–3275). Nearby, exhibits in the *Peary-MacMillan Arctic Museum* (207–725–3416) outline the history of polar expeditions and display belongings of these two arctic explorers.

Travel along the central Maine coast from Portland to Bar Harbor has always been easier by sea than by land. For a glimpse of unspoiled Maine, you must be willing to drive up and down the necks. Here you'll find old saltwater farms, their land split between two or three necks (the dory was as important a tool as the plow), and small coves with lobster-men's houses and piers.

The Harpswells

To see some of this country, drive down Route 123 from Brunswick along *Harpswell Neck,* a narrow finger into the sea, 1½ miles across at its widest point. In the tiny village of *Harpswell Center* the 1757 *First Meetinghouse* is a fine example of early church architecture.

The area abounds with legends. You may see a headless horseman rid-ing through *South Harpswell.* Come at midnight when the moon is bright. Or you might catch the *Ghost Ship of Harpswell,* fully rigged and under sail. That ship is part of a tragic legend about two young friends, George Leverett and Charles Jose, who fell in love with Sara Soule. Jose left town, while Leverett stayed and built a ship he named the *Sarah*. He sailed into Portland to pick up cargo, and there saw a ship armed with a cannon. It was the *Don Pedro*, and it was sailed by his rival, Jose. The *Don Pedro* attacked, and all on board the *Sarah* were killed except Leverett; he was tied to the mast of his ship, and she was pushed out to sea.

According to the legend, the *Sarah's* dead crew set sail and turned the ship toward home. The ghostly crew took Leverett ashore and left him with his logbook on the beach, where he was rescued. The *Sarah* was sighted from **Harpswell House** in 1880. She gleamed in the sun, headed straight for the harbor, and then disappeared, as though she'd come home for the last time.

Orr's Island/Bailey Island

North of Harpswell Center on Route 123 there's a road heading east that takes you to Route 24. Head south through the area of another local legend, where a murdered pirate supposedly stands guard over buried treasure (some say they've seen his light or heard him moaning). Between Orr's Island and Bailey Island, separated by Will's Gut, there's an uncemented granite-block bridge that's laid out like a honeycomb so that the tides and rushing spring thaws can flow through freely. You'll see a statue of a Maine lobsterman at **Land's End** on the tip of Bailey Island. After a storm, when the surf is high, or any time, take the cliff walk for superb views of **Casco Bay** and **Halfway Rock Light.**

FOR MORE INFORMATION

Chamber of Commerce of the Bath-Brunswick Region, 59 Pleasant Street, Brunswick, ME 04011; (207) 725–8797; www.midcoastmaine.com

Freeport Merchants Association, 23 Depot Street, P.O. Box 452, Freeport, ME 04032; (800) 865–1994 or (207) 865–1212; www.freeportusa.com

Portland Convention and Visitor's Bureau, 305 Commercial Street, Portland, ME 04101; (207) 772–5800; www.visitportland.com

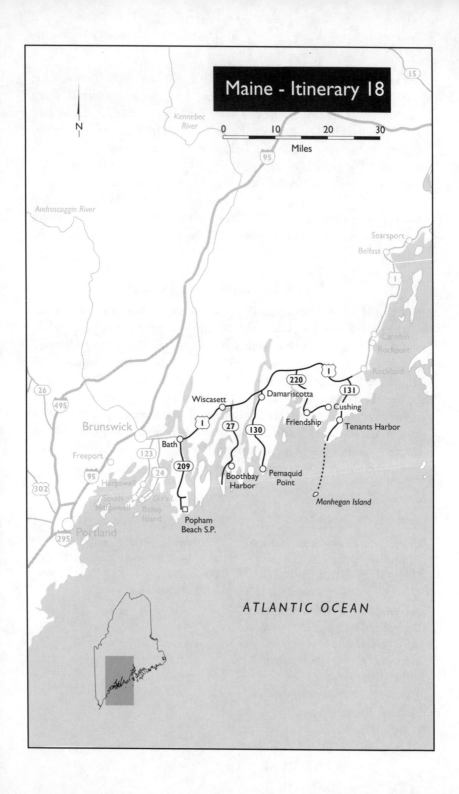

ITINERARY 18

Bath • Popham Beach • Wiscasset
Boothbay Harbor • Damariscotta • Pemaquid Point
Friendship • Cushing/Tenants Harbor

Bath

Head back up Route 24 and take Route 1 east into Bath, Maine's cradle of shipbuilding. Some 5,000 vessels have been launched here, including half of all the wooden sailing vessels built in the United States between 1862 and 1902.

The *Maine Maritime Museum* (Washington Street, 207–443–1316) is located on the site of a nineteenth-century shipyard. Exhibits in Sewall Hall are attractively arranged, interspersing ship models, paintings, and artifacts with focused displays such as "Ports of Call: Maine Seafarers' Voyage the World."

The *Percy and Small Shipyard* is the focus of the museum, and there are a number of sites to visit. Buildings on the grounds include the Boat Shop, where the fragrant smell of sawdust shavings wafts over volunteers and staff building and restoring watercraft. The deck below contains a variety of historic craft from years past. The Paint and Treenail Shop contains a model of a ropewalk. Another building houses an exhibit on lobstering, including a collection of early lobster traps and boats. When the ships are in port, visitors may go on board the Grand Banks schooner *Sherman Zwicker* to learn about cod fishing, or take a ride on the *Schoodic* to see the Kennebec River shoreline from the water.

Popham Beach

From Bath, take Route 209 south to Popham Beach to visit the site of *Popham Colony,* where a hundred English colonists arrived in 1607. Discouraged by the harsh winter and sickness, they stayed just a year, most of them returning to England on the *Virginia*, a ship they built themselves (the very first made in America).

At the *Fort Popham Memorial* (see below) you'll see the partial construction of a fort that was begun in 1861 and never finished. Displays here interpret the history of the area—the story of Popham Colony, Benedict Arnold's march through Maine, and the fort's construction.

The memorial is in **Popham Beach State Park** (Route 209, 207–389–1335), a facility extending along 4½ miles of fine sand. There are tidal pools, dunes, rocky outcroppings, and warm water (for Maine). Come early; parking is limited.

Wiscasset

Continue up Route 1 to Wiscasset, one of the prettiest villages in Maine. **Castle Tucker** (Lee and High Streets, 207–882–7169), where you'll find a freestanding elliptical staircase, has a beautiful view overlooking Wiscasset Harbor. It's furnished with original Victorian pieces. Many of the furnishings in the **Nickels-Sortwell House** (Main and Federal Streets, 207–882–6218) are also originals.

The **Musical Wonder House** (18 High Street, 800–336–3725) has an unusual collection of music boxes, player pianos, gramophones, pipe organs, and period antiques.

Stop at the **Maine Art Gallery** on Warren Street (207–882–7511). The gallery features work by local artists and hosts a special show during the summer.

One of our favorite sites has disappeared. In 1998 the remains of the *Luther Little* and the *Hesper,* two four-masted schooners that had been rotting in the harbor tidal flats since 1932, were removed by the town. The likeness of the ships—picturesque reminders of the last days of commercial sailing—serves as the town symbol and the logo for many Wiscasset business.

Boothbay Harbor

Boothbay Harbor is on Route 27, south of Wiscasset. It's one of the finest and busiest of Maine's natural harbors, with commercial fishing boats, excursion boats, windjammers, and deep-sea fishing charters going in and out. In mid-July the harbor is the site of the three-day **Windjammer Festival,** but you can see these marvelous sailing ships here all summer long.

At the **Boothbay Railway Village** (Route 27; 207–633–4727), you'll find antique cars and fire equipment, railroad society memorabilia, and a collection of antique dolls. When you're through exploring, take a ride on a narrow-gauge railroad.

For more information about the town, stop at the chamber of commerce or the ***Boothbay Region Historical Society*** (207–633–0820) on Townsend Avenue.

Damariscotta

Return to Route 1 and continue eastward to Damariscotta. Stop at the visitors' center on Main Street, then cross the street to the ***Chapman-Hall House*** (207–882–6172). It was built in 1754 and is furnished with period pieces. Also here you will find a collection of eighteenth-century tools (crafts, farming, and shipbuilding) and an herb garden.

Pemaquid Point

Are you longing for the coast proper? Head south on Route 130 to Pemaquid Point. ***Pemaquid Point Lighthouse,*** which towers over the pounding surf, is a glorious spot for spending time. Enjoy the magnificent view, then visit the ***Fisherman's Museum*** (207–677–2494) in the lightkeeper's house next door.

If you enjoy archeological digs, ***Colonial Pemaquid Historic Site*** (207–677–2423) is the place to go. Foundations dating from the early seventeenth-century settlement have been uncovered. You can see artifacts, including household pieces and farming implements, in the adjacent museum.

Fort William Henry (207–677–2423) is a replica of the second of three English forts on the site. The tower of the fort contains artifacts found on the site, military equipment, and Indian deeds. The ***Old Fort Cemetery,*** just outside the grounds, contains old slate stones marking graves, including that of Ann Rodgers, wife of Lieutenant Patrick Rodgers, who died in 1758.

You may wonder about this bit of graffiti found during a church restoration in Pemaquid. Someone wrote, "McLain is a lying fool" and placed it on a plaster layer under the ***Harrington Meeting House*** (Old Harrington Road, 207–677–2246). The Reverend Alexander McLain came to America in 1770 and traveled on horseback to service each of the three meeting houses—apparently to a mixed response. A historical museum now occupies the gallery area. It houses artifacts, tools, maps, period clothing, and documents contributed by local residents. The Harrington Burial Ground contains stones dating back to 1716.

Friendship

Return to Route 1, head east, and take Route 220 south to Friendship, home of the famous Friendship Sloop. For the town's *Yearbook and Guide* contact *Maine Sunshine, Inc.* (43 Park Street, Rockland, ME 04841; 207–594–8074 or 800–948–4337).

The *Friendship Sloop Society* schedules a number of rendezvous and races during the summer. *Friendship Sloop Days* are held in Rockland in mid-July.

Cushing/Tenants Harbor

From Friendship, meander through the countryside to Cushing, where Andrew Wyeth summered and painted. The *Olson House* here, once the home of Christina Olson, is now administered by the Farnsworth Art Museum (see Rockland) and is open to the public. Andrew Wyeth made this site famous in his well-known painting *Christina's World,* which was part of a series. For information about the Olson House, contact the *Farnsworth Art Museum* (207–596–6457).

You will pass through *Thomaston,* a village of beautiful sea captains' homes on Route 1. Then go south on Route 131 to Tenants Harbor, a lovely fishing village out of the mainstream. There you will find more summer residents and sailors than tourists. And you can stop for a swim in the magnificent clear quarry.

Side Trip–Monhegan Island

Just beyond Tenants Harbor, from Port Clyde, you can join the mailboat *Laura B* (207–372–8848) to reach Monhegan Island, which lies 9 miles out to sea, or you can take the ferry (a more comfortable ride). *Balmy Days II* (207–633–2284) runs from Boothbay Harbor, June through September. Leif Erikson may have landed here in the year 1000, and we know that John Cabot did in 1498. Later Monhegan was a haven for pirates.

You can't bring your car, but the island is only a couple of miles long and a mile wide and the views along the rugged cliffs on the offshore side are well worth the walk. While you're exploring, plan a stop at the *Monhegan Museum,* in the former lightkeepers' house. What's here? Indian artifacts, exhibits about the island's wildlife, and an art gallery.

FOR MORE INFORMATION

Bath Business Association, PMB 10 State Road, Suite 9, Bath, ME 04530; (207) 443–9702; www.visitbath.com

Boothbay Harbor Region Chamber of Commerce, Route 27, 192 Townsend Avenue, P.O. Box 356, Boothbay Harbor, ME 04538; (800) 266–8422 or (207) 633–2353; www.boothbayharbor.com

Damariscotta Region Chamber of Commerce, Courtyard Street, P.O. Box 13, Damariscotta, ME 04543; (207) 563–8340; www.drcc.org

Pemaquid Area Association, 301 State Route 32, Pemaquid, ME 04541; (207) 677–2246

Wiscasset Regional Business Association, P.O. Box 150, Wiscasset, ME 04578; (207) 882–4600; www.wiscassetmaine.com

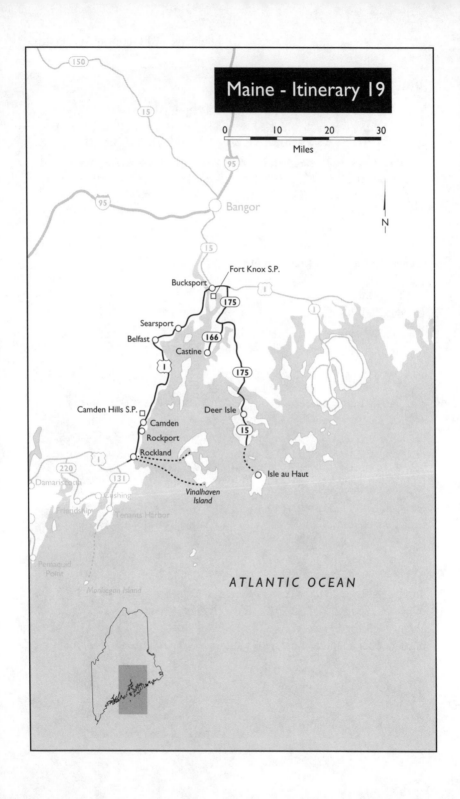

Maine - Itinerary 19

0   10   20   30
Miles

150

15

95

Bangor

15

Fort Knox S.P.

Bucksport

175

Searsport

Belfast

166

Castine

1

175

Camden Hills S.P.

Camden

Deer Isle

Rockport

15

Rockland

220

131

Damariscotta

Cushing

Isle au Haut

Friendship

Vinalhaven
Island

Tenants Harbor

Pemaquid
Point

Monhegan Island

ATLANTIC OCEAN

N

ITINERARY 19

Rockland • Rockport • Camden • Belfast • Searsport
Bucksport • Castine • Deer Isle • Isle au Haut

Rockland

Follow Route 1 east to Rockland, where you'll find the ***William A. Farnsworth Library and Art Museum*** (352 Main Street, 207–596–6457). The Farnsworth Art Museum features an impressive collection of Maine-inspired artists and has now expanded to include five buildings in Rockland.

The Museum's ***Center for the Wyeth Family*** houses an extensive collection of art by the talented Wyeths, including N.C. Wyeth, Andrew Wyeth, and Jamie Wyeth. Also in the museum's collection are the works of other nineteenth- and twentieth-century artists, among them Winslow Homer, Fitz Hugh Lane, Gilbert Stuart, and Thomas Eakins. The ***Farnsworth Homestead*** is adjacent to the museum.

The ***Owls Head Transportation Museum*** (P.O. Box 277, Route 73, Owls Head, ME 04854; 207–594–4418) offers a collection of antique aircraft, automobiles, and engines including World War I fighter planes, a Stanley Steamer, and a Model T Ford.

Rockland is the departure point for eight of Maine's fleet of traditional windjammers, now carrying passengers on coastal cruises rather than freight from port to port. Captains Douglas and Linda Lee, after decades of rebuilding and sailing older Maine schooners, conceived and designed the 94-foot ***Heritage*** (800–648–4544), built her with their own hands, and have been her co-captains since she was launched in 1983. At the time, they explained, "The new schooner was not to be a replica of any specific traditional vessel. She will be the next generation of coasting schooner adapted to meet the cargo-carrying requirements of today—which is you and me."

Side Trip–Vinalhaven

The *State of Maine Ferry Service* (207–596–2202) runs boats between Rockland and the island of Vinalhaven. On the island, one of the oldest summer colonies in New England, you'll find a number of interesting houses. Also here: a marvelous area for cruising and an active fishing industry. Stop for a swim in one of the spring-filled granite quarries, explore a small cove, or just sit back and enjoy the view. Across a small strip of water to the north, you can see North Haven Island, and to the southwest sits Hurricane Island, where the first Outward Bound School was located.

Rockport

Heading up the west shore of Penobscot Bay on Route 1 you come to Rockport, former summer home of *André the Seal,* who was memorialized in the film *Andre.* This seal used to swim 160 miles to Boston to spend the winter at the aquarium there, and then back to Maine again in the spring. His keeper, Harry Goodridge, taught him a number of tricks, which he performed afternoons in his special floating pen near the head of the harbor. André died in 1986, but there's a statue in his memory at the marine park in Rockport.

Also in the marine park stand three partially restored lime kilns, which used to have active lives as part of a local industry. A roaring fire produced a lime concentrate from limestone, for use in plastering. The extract was put in sealed barrels and then into vessels. The cargo was considered dangerous as it could ignite.

When you're ready to eat, try the *Ski Loft* (Public Landing, 207–236–2330) for a meal with a view of Rockport's fine harbor.

Camden

Continue up Route 1 from Rockport to Camden, one of Maine's most interesting towns. The harbor is a fascinating place, busy with commercial and charter fishing boats, sloops, and a large fleet of windjammers (offering weekly cruises). For information on windjammer cruises, contact the *Maine Windjammer Association* (P.O. Box 1144, Blue Hill, ME 04614; 800–807–9463).

Stop at the **Camden Information Booth** (Public Landing, 207–236–4404) for a wealth of information about the area. Then enjoy the shops and restaurants and the view of the waterfalls running through the center of town.

Merryspring (Conway Road, 207–236–2239) is a sixty-six-acre garden designed to let you appreciate Maine's indigenous plant life. An arboretum, a woodland garden, a pond, herb and lily gardens, and raised flower beds are all connected by trails.

Conway Homestead and Mary Meeker Cramer Museum (Conway Road, 207–236–2257) dates from 1770, with later additions in 1815 and 1825. The house has roof timbers fastened with treenails, or trunnels. Some of the beams in the cellar are still covered with bark, and there is a bake-oven built with small bricks in the kitchen. The entrance hall is curved and contains a "parson's cupboard."

The complex also includes a blacksmith shop, herb garden, maple sugar house, and barn. The barn houses a collection of carriages, sleighs, farm tools, and a saw to cut ice. The Mary Meeker Cramer Museum houses collections of antique glass, paintings, musical instruments, furniture, costumes, quilts, and ship models.

Camden is nestled against the **Camden Hills,** which rise majestically from the shore of the bay. Come for the view or the hiking—both are exceptional. The **Mount Battie South Trail** begins at the end of Megunticook Street (north of the town square). The 1-mile path is steep, but the views from the ledges are worth the climb. Or take the easy way to the top (800 feet): the toll road from **Camden Hills State Park** (Route 1, 207–236–3109).

Mount Megunticook Trail (1½ miles to the summit) begins at the warden's hut in the park's campgrounds. Enjoy beautiful views of the ocean as you wind your way up to the summit of Mount Megunticook, the highest of the Camden Hills (1,385 feet); then come down the **Tablelands Trail** to Mount Battie Road.

We suggest an alternate route if you're short of time. From the ranger hut on Mount Battie Road in Camden Hills State Park, drive up to the Tablelands parking lot. Hike along the Tablelands Trail up Mount Megunticook to **Ocean Lookout.** The hike is 1 mile and takes fifty minutes at a reasonable pace. Rocks at the top are perfect for relaxing with a snack while taking in the view. The trails are marked with white slashes and also with brown signs at junctions. We recommend hiking boots because of rough stones. After the hike you can drive the rest of the way up the road to the tower on Mount Battie for more views.

Bald Rock Mountain Trail starts 4 miles north of the park, on Route 1. (Look for a sign near telephone pole 106.) Follow yellow blazes along a logging trail to Bald Rock Summit (1,100 feet), where there are shelters if you want to spend the night. On a clear day you can see Northport, Lincolnville, Islesboro Island, Deer Isle, and even Pulpit Harbor on North Haven. The trail is 3 miles long.

Maiden Cliff, named for an eleven-year-old girl who fell to her death in May 1864, offers spectacular views of Megunticook Lake and the surrounding countryside. Follow Route 52 west from Camden to the Barrett Place parking lot, where the *Maiden Cliff Trail* begins. At the summit (1,024 feet)—it's marked by a wooden cross—pick up the *Scenic Trail* for your return trip. The total distance is 2½ miles.

Ragged Mountain Trail begins at the Camden Ski Bowl (take John Street from town) and continues up the lift line, turns right into the woods, and runs along the ridge to the summit (1,300 feet). You can see the ocean over Oyster River Pond, the Glen Cove area, and Maiden Cliff. Then come down any of the ski runs.

For fine seafood dining in town, try *Cappy's Chowder House* (1 Main Street, 207–236–2254), *The Waterfront* (Bay View Street, 207–236–3747), or the *Lobster Pound* (Route 1 in Lincolnville, 207–789–5550). Then head north on Route 1 to Belfast and Searsport.

Belfast

If you, like Thoreau, yearn to spend time in an unspoiled part of Maine, you'll enjoy Waldo County, stretching westward from the upper west shore of Penobscot Bay and the lower Penobscot River. According to an Indian aphorism, the region is "2 or 3 miles up the river, one beautiful country."

In 1838 Henry David Thoreau headed up the Penobscot River and found that out for himself. This land, tucked between Camden and Acadia National Park, is less well known than either of those tourist attractions. It has changed very little in the past 150 years and is home to Down Easters who wouldn't live anywhere else.

Today, walkers and hikers come to enjoy shady wooded trails and headlands with familiar Penobscot views, which include lobstermen tending traps and Maine schooners putting in and out of the harbors. Sailing yachts tack back and forth and kayakers paddle slowly out to a pristine beach for a swim and a picnic. Seafood buffs find lobster rolls almost everywhere or feast on whole steamed lobsters at pierside restaurants.

Several of the county's principal towns, notably Belfast and Searsport, have taken pains to preserve their heritage. You can pick up a brochure at the chamber of commerce (see page 117) for the *Historic Walking Tour of Belfast*, a town with a treasure trove of period homes.

Stroll along Church Street, beginning at the *First Church*, a building with a history dating from 1819, when an organ on its way to the church was lost at sea but later replaced. Look for the burned board near the left front pew, which was probably caused by a foot warmer. Several Federal houses along the route date from the 1820s and 1830s. Don't miss the *Henry Moore House* (One Depot Square) and its beautiful garden at the rear of the house.

Passengers of all ages will enjoy a leisurely round-trip train ride from Belfast to Brooks on the *Belfast & Moosehead Lake Railroad Company* (One Depot Square, 800–392–5500 or 207–948–5500). You can move through the cars to a diner or an open viewing car if you don't mind a little rocking and rolling on this historic roadbed. If you have children with you, have them watch out for a masked man as the train nears Waldo Station!

For a marine perspective, you can paddle your own tandem kayak from *Belfast Kayak Tours* (207–382–6204), either with an experienced guide or independently. Inexperienced participants learn how to hold their paddles with hands properly spaced and to execute various strokes. Easy and relaxed, we glided through the anchorage past a double-ended cruising sloop, lobster boats, a catamaran, an ocean-racing sloop, a cruising yawl, and a fleet of day sailors. Farther along the shore we explored several coves, paddling into shallow sections that only kayaks can reach.

In this maritime community you can have lobster every day if you wish, as well as other regional specialties. In Belfast try the *Weathervane Restaurant* (Public Landing, 207–338–1774), *Belfast Co-op Cafe* (123 High Street, 207–338–2532), or *Belfast Bay Brew Pub and Restaurant* (100 Searsport Avenue, 207–338–2662). In Lincolnville the *Youngtown Inn & Restaurant* (Route 52, 207–763–4290) provides fine dining, while the *Lobster Pound Restaurant* (207–789–5550) is more informal.

Searsport

From Belfast head east a few miles on Route 1 to Searsport. There the impressive *Penobscot Marine Museum* (Church Street, 207–548–2529) includes eight buildings at the heart of this port town: an 1860 Captain's Home, the 1845 Town Hall, houses dating from 1825 and 1880, and a sea captain's home housing antique furnishings, models, paintings, a glass collection, memorabilia, and a modern research library.

Several figureheads greet visitors at the door of the *Old Town Hall.* When we visited, a group of children were admiring two Fu dogs (traditional Chinese good luck sculptures) brought back from China. In sailing-ship days, captain's wives often lived on board with their husbands and children. One display features a photograph of "Joanna" at fourteen months; she was born at sea on board the *Charlotte A. Littlefield*. Captain Phineas Banning Blanchard's ship models are also on display. As a model builder he is renowned, with good reason.

The highly valued Thomas and James Buttersworth paintings are on the second floor of the *Captain Jeremiah Merithew House.* Our favorites include *British Frigate and Brig off a Lighthouse, Clipper Ship* Nebraska, Sea Horse *Capturing* La Sensible, and *Naval Battle Between HMS* Shannon *and USS* Chesapeake.

Searsport's *Rhumb Line Restaurant* (207–548–2600) is building a reputation for its cuisine.

Castine

From Searsport continue on Route 1 through Bucksport to Route 175 heading south, then continue on Routes 166 and 166A on the Naskeag peninsula. Here you'll reach Castine, a quiet town with a stormy history. In 1779 Commodore Saltonstall led Paul Revere and other patriots here in the Massachusetts Expedition. The expedition—a mission to dislodge the British from their base at Castine—failed miserably, and all the American boats were lost. Because the unsuccessful mission was such an embarrassment to several prominent patriots, it was never fully documented. And the British? They occupied the town again during the War of 1812.

You can learn more about the area's history at *Fort George* (Wadsworth Cove Road), where fortifications were constructed as early as 1626. The buildings have been razed and rebuilt many times since. Then stroll around the town, reading the historical markers and enjoying the fine examples of colonial architecture. Call Bucksport Bay Area Chamber of Commerce (207–469–6818) or Castine Historic Preservation (207–326–8071) for information about Fort George.

Side Trip–Fort Knox State Park

From Searsport continue east on Route 1 to *Fort Knox State Park,* just across the river from Bucksport. *Fort Knox* (207–469–7719), dating from 1844, is a massive stone fortress overlooking a strategic narrows near the mouth of the Penobscot River. The central fort, a polygon in shape, is protected by outer walls and still retains waterfront batteries with some of the original cannons in place. Major General Henry Knox was head of artillery under George Washington. You can climb to the parapets, visit the dungeons, and take a walk through "two-step alley," but be careful because it is almost completely dark along this counterscarf protecting the inner fort. Telephone ahead to find out when reenactments are held.

Wilson Museum (Perkins Street, 207–326–8753) contains anthropological and geological collections as well as colonial pieces. The *John Perkins House,* dating from 1763, is on the grounds. As the only pre-Revolutionary building in the region, it holds historical interest with its hand-hewn beams. The house contains eighteenth-century pieces, and some date from the Perkins family. Artifacts given by local inhabitants are on display, and interpreters demonstrate the work done in the blacksmith shop. Don't overlook the interesting collection in the *Hearse House.*

The *Maine Maritime Academy* (207–326–4311) offers tours of the *State of Maine,* a training ship. In August the academy also schedules nature walks with staff members. These field trips on the natural history of the seashore last between two and three hours.

From Castine retrace your route on Routes 166 and 199 until you meet Route 175, then head south again. On your way down the Penobscot peninsula to Deer Isle, stop at North Brooksville on Route 175, where a bridge crosses over a rapids in the Bagaduce River. These rapids reverse with the tide. About 2 miles downriver is another reversing rapids, more vigorous than the first, where the current passes through a narrow rocky channel. You can launch a canoe or small boat near the bridge and run the rapids, either up or down the river, depending on the tide.

The stretch of river between the two rapids is a haven for seals. Come on a fine day at low tide and you'll see them sunning on uncovered rocks.

Deer Isle

Continue on Route 175 to Route 15, crossing *Eggemoggin Reach* on a high suspension bridge. Deer Isle is a great area for exploring and discovering something new and interesting around the next bend. What's here? Towns climbing into the hills, harbors active with lobstering, and scallop and sardine catches; historic homes; a musicians' retreat; an abandoned silver mine; a granite quarry; lilies floating on Ames Pond; highly skilled craftspeople; and mounds of shells left by the Indians.

Isle au Haut

From Stonington, at the tip of Deer Isle, you can take the mailboat to Isle au Haut, 6 miles out to sea and a part of Acadia National Park. Named by Samuel de Champlain in 1604 for its high land, the island is relatively untouched, with just a few roads and trails around the perimeter. Bring your bike or plan to hike.

FOR MORE INFORMATION

Belfast Chamber of Commerce,
29 Front Street, P.O. Box 58, Belfast,
ME 04915; (207) 338–5900;
www.belfastmaine.org

**Bucksport Bay Area Chamber of
Commerce,** 231 Main Street,
P.O. Box 1880, Bucksport, ME 04416;
(207) 469–6818

**Camden-Rockport-Lincolnville
Chamber of Commerce,** Commercial
Street, Public Landing, P.O. Box 919,
Camden, ME 04843; (800) 223–5459
or (207) 236–4404; visitcamden.com

**Deer Isle-Stonington Chamber of
Commerce,** P.O. Box 459, Stonington,
ME 04681; (207) 348–6124

**Rockland-Thomaston Area
Chamber of Commerce,**
Harbor Park, P.O. Box 508, Rockland,
ME 04841; (800) 562–2529 or
(207) 596–0376; midcoast. com/~rtacc

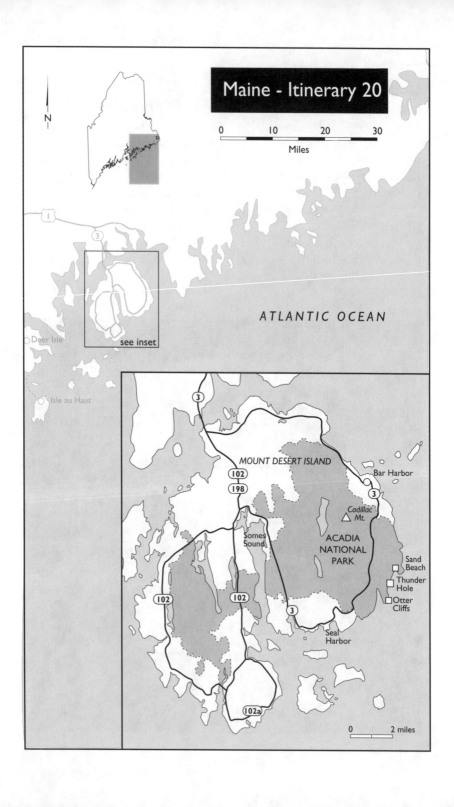

ITINERARY 20

Bar Harbor • Acadia National Park

From the Deer Isle bridge, meander up to Ellsworth through the Brooklin and Blue Hill regions, using Routes 175 and 176 (if you have time for some pleasant circuits) to 172; then take Route 3 from Ellsworth to the Mount Desert Island bridge.

This beautiful island was discovered by Champlain, who named it *l'Isle des Monts Déserts* because the mountains looked so barren. In 1613 a group of Jesuits settled on Fernald's Point but were driven out by the British after only a month. That skirmish was the first in a century and a half of fighting between French and British for control of this area.

Today almost half of the island (along with parts of two nearby islands) makes up *Acadia National Park* (see below). The terrain is varied—wooded valleys, lakes, mountains, and granite shore constantly lashed by the sea—and filled with beautiful trees and wildflowers, birds, and other animals. If you want to get a sea view of the island, take a cruise from *Bar Harbor Whale Watch Co.* (207–288–3322) in Bar Harbor.

Bar Harbor

Bar Harbor is the largest and best known town on Mount Desert Island. At one time a fabulous summer resort, many of the elegant nineteenth-century "cottages" were destroyed in a disastrous fire in 1947. To see some of the remaining cottages, walk along the coastal path from the park behind the public landing, past the Bar Harbor Inn. Plan to spend some time looking around this interesting town, which has a diversity of shops, galleries, and boutiques, then select one of the many good restaurants for lunch or dinner. *Duffy's Quarterdeck Restaurant* (207–288–5292) is located right on the corner of Main Street, with great water views. Local friends recommend *Testa's Restaurant* (207–288–3327), *Galyn's Galley* (207–288–9706), the *Chart Room* (207–288–9740), the *Bar Harbor Inn* (207–288–3351), and the *Island Chowder House* (207–288–4905).

Acadia National Park

Begin your visit with a stop at the *Visitor's Center* at the *Hulls Cove park entrance* to find maps, guidebooks, and information about trails (hiking and biking), self-guided nature walks, and special programs. A tour of the park? *Ollie's Trolley* (207–288–3327) or *Acadia National Park Tours* (207–288–4728) in Bar Harbor offer a bus trip around the park. Or you can rent a tape recorder and taped tour at the visitors' center, and drive yourself.

The *Acadia Park Loop Road* begins north of Bar Harbor on Route 3 at the Hull's Cove entrance, which you will have passed on the way to town. You can also get onto the loop road from town at the *Cadillac Mountain entrance* or the *Sieur de Monts entrance.* The northern section of the road has several scenic overlooks that offer magnificent views of Frenchman Bay and Bar Harbor itself. Just beyond the Cadillac Mountain entrance, the road becomes one way, which allows you to stop in the right lane to enjoy the views. *Sieur de Monts Spring,* farther out, has a nature center and a wildflower garden. Nearby, the *Abbe Museum* (207–288–3519) preserves the Native American history of the area.

Hardy souls can stop for a swim at *Sand Beach,* where the average temperature of the water in summer is a brisk 50 to 55 degrees. There is some surf, although the beach is in a protected cove. Those who prefer exercising on their feet can explore the trails on *Great Head* adjoining the beach.

A bit farther along the road, don't miss *Thunder Hole,* where the waves crash in and out with a roar when there is any sea running. And don't fail to stop at *Otter Cliffs*—the highest headlands on the East Coast —where the view is indeed spectacular. As you continue along the Park Loop Road, it turns northward and becomes Jordan Pond Road. Soon you'll come to *Jordan Pond House,* which is a great place for lunch, tea, or dinner (207–276–3316).

As you drive along the Atlantic shore, you can see *Cadillac Mountain* rising from the interior. You can reach the 1,530-foot mountain, the highest point on the Atlantic coast north of Rio de Janeiro, by continuing north on Jordan Pond Road until you reach the turnoff for Cadillac Mountain. From the summit you can see sparkling *Eagle Lake* to the northwest and *Somes Sound* to the west. The sound, the only natural fjord on the East Coast, creeps in so far that the island is almost cut in two.

Swimmers: Besides Sand Beach mentioned above, try *Seal Harbor Beach,* a community beach off Route 3 not far south of the loop road, where the water temperature hovers around fifty-seven degrees in summer. The surf is gentle, the drop-off gradual. There is also a beach with warmer water at the south end of *Echo Lake,* off Route 102. But if you're exploring the island's coast by boat, there's an even better place to swim. When we anchored off Somesville at the inner end of Somes Sound once, we found perfect swimming in water that was actually warm enough for us to stay in half an hour—an extended swim almost unheard of on the Maine coast.

For walkers, hikers, riders, and cyclists, Mount Desert is pure paradise. *Carriage paths* were built by John D. Rockefeller for the pleasure of summer guests. Now they are wonderful for cycling, horseback riding, and easy walking. There are also self-guided nature trails at Jordan Pond (½ mile in length) and at Ship Harbor, off Route 102A south of Southwest Harbor (1½ miles).

The Park Visitor Center has maps and trail information for hiking. Ask for the sheet that rates the difficulty of hikes. Here is a selection. We especially enjoyed one from the east end of Sand Beach that circles Great Head in larger and smaller loops (1½ miles total) over rock headlands with fine views (moderate rating). The *Ocean Trail* also stretches from Sand Beach to Otter Point (3½ miles) along the cliffs below the road (easy rating).

At the eastern end of the island you can walk Champlain Mountain from south to north on the *Gorham Mountain Trail* and a variety of linked trails to the north. The 6-mile trail begins a mile north of Otter Cliffs at the Monument Cove parking area. The *South Ridge Trail* (7 miles) takes you to the summit of Cadillac Mountain; it begins at the campground on Otter Cove. Shorter trails to the top include the *West Face Trail* from Jordan Pond Road and the *North Ridge Trail* from the Bar Harbor side of Ocean Drive. Other trails extend from the summit through the bowl and up to the ridge of Champlain Mountain. But watch out for cars as you cross Route 3!

Pemetic Mountain Trail, an easy 2 miles, begins at the north end of Bubble Pond, off Jordan Pond Road, and goes along the ridge to the top of Pemetic Mountain (1,248 feet).

The Penobscot and Sargent Mountains run along the west side of Jordan Pond. The *Jordan Pond Shore Path* is an easy 3½-mile loop. The *Jordan Cliffs Trail* begins at the Jordan Pond House; the distance, if you circle back on the Penobscot Mountain Trail, is about 5 miles. You can enjoy long views over Blue Hill Bay, the Atlantic, even Frenchman's Bay; then stop for lunch on your way out.

Norumbega Mountain Trail begins on Route 198 near Upper Hadlock Pond and extends almost 3 miles. From the top (852 feet) you can see Southwest Harbor and Tremont. Be sure to bring along a pail or a basket if you're hiking in blueberry season.

On the west side of Somes Sound, the *Acadia Mountain Trail* offers an easy walk through an area rich in history. An early French colony was formed here on Saint Sauveur Mountain but was later destroyed by the English. English patrols used to come to *Man o' War Brook* to fill their casks with fresh water and to hunt and fish. The trail is 2½ miles long and begins on Robinson Road, off Route 102, across from Echo Lake. Look for the sign to the summit (644 feet).

FOR MORE INFORMATION

Acadia National Park, P.O. Box 177, Bar Harbor, ME 04609; (207) 288–3338; www.nps.gov/acad

Bar Harbor Chamber of Commerce, 93 Cottage Street, P.O. Box 158, Bar Harbor, ME 04609; (800) 288–5103 or (207) 288–5103; www.barharborinfo.com

ITINERARY 21

Sebago Lake • Paris • Bethel • Rangeley Lakes
Moosehead Lake • Baxter State Park

Many people think of Maine in terms of the coastline alone, but the vast interior of the state contains a multitude of crystal clear lakes, several mountain ranges, and more untroubled wilderness than the rest of New England put together. Vacationers can enjoy this part of Maine year-round, with water sports, fishing, and hiking in the summer and skiing in the winter. Families find that camping by lakes and mountains makes vacations affordable and memorable.

Major lake regions include those around Sebago Lake, the Rangeley Lakes, Moosehead Lake, and the Allagash Wilderness Waterway. The Longfellow Mountains run from Rangeley all the way to Baxter State Park. A final itinerary and some side trips take you inland to Maine's vast stretches of forest, punctuated by pristine lakes for fishing and imposing mountains for skiing or climbing. Our route begins in the Sebago Lake region to the south and wanders northward and eastward through the mountains all the way to Baxter State Park. You can combine any part of this itinerary with seacoast pleasures by connecting to any of the previous itineraries.

Sebago Lake

Maine's second-largest lake is a resort community especially famous for its landlocked salmon, as well as squaretail trout, tongue, and black bass. There are villages around the shores offering accommodations, and camping is available in *Sebago Lake State Park* (11 Park Access Road, Route 302, Casco, ME 04015; 207–693–6231). Antiques and craft shops dot the area.

Nearby on Douglas Hill, the *Jones Gallery of Glass and Ceramics* (207–787–3370) houses an extensive collection built up over the years by Dorothy Jones. The museum offers changing exhibits, a gallery shop that includes some antique pieces, tours, a lecture program, and a library.

Two miles south of the lake in Standish, the *Daniel Marrett House* (207–436–3205) played an important part in the War of 1812. Fearing that the British would capture Portland, the town fathers took money from

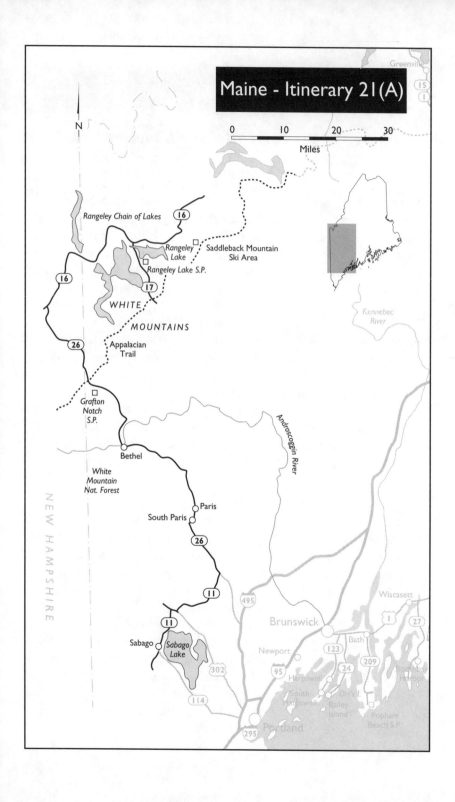

Maine - Itinerary 21(A)

0   10   20   30

Miles

N

Greenville

15

1

Rangeley Chain of Lakes

16

Rangeley Lake

Rangeley Lake S.P.

Saddleback Mountain Ski Area

17

WHITE

16

MOUNTAINS

26

Appalacian Trail

Kennebec River

Grafton Notch S.P.

Androscoggin River

Bethel

White Mountain Nat. Forest

Paris

South Paris

26

11

495

NEW HAMPSHIRE

11

Sabago

Sabago Lake

302

114

Wiscasett

1

27

Brunswick

Bath

Newport

123

209

95

24

Harpswell

South Harpswell

Orr's I.

Bailey Island

Popham Beach S.P.

295

Portland

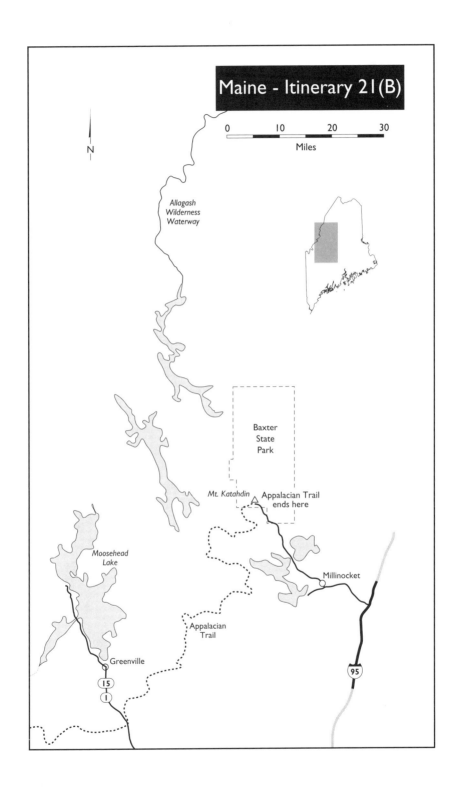

Maine - Itinerary 21(B)

0   10   20   30
Miles

N

Allagash
Wilderness
Waterway

Baxter
State
Park

Mt. Katahdin   Appalacian Trail
ends here

Moosehead
Lake

Millinocket

Appalacian
Trail

Greenville

15

1

95

Portland banks and stored it in the house. This part-Georgian, part-Greek Revival home is furnished with eighteenth- and nineteenth-century family furniture.

Hikers recommend the view from the top of *Douglas Mountain.* At 1,415 feet you can see Sebago Lake, the surrounding lakes, and the White Mountains of New Hampshire.

Route 25 west and Route 11 southwest to Newfield lead you to *Willowbrook at Newfield* (207–793–2784), a restored nineteenth-century village. Twenty-seven buildings house a "trades of yesteryear" exhibit, restored sleighs and carriages, tools, and farm implements.

Just north of Sebago Lake sits *Songo Lock,* built in 1830 as part of the Cumberland–Oxford Canal from Portland to Harrison. Songo Lock connects Sebago Lake with Long Lake to the northwest. It's fun to help open or close the hand-operated lock or just watch the procedure. The Songo River flows between Sebago Lake and Long Lake, extending the range for sailors and boaters. If you didn't bring a boat, you can take a cruise on the Mississippi River paddlewheeler, *Songo River Queen II* (207–693–6861), located on Route 302 at the causeway in Naples, or help deliver the mail on the U.S. mail boat from the causeway.

Paris

Head northeast from Sebago Lake on Route 11 and north on Route 26 to the *Shaker Museum* (207–926–4597) in Paris, a living-history museum that portrays Shaker life from the eighteenth century to the present day. The Sabbathday Lake Shaker community was founded in 1783 and formally established in 1794. The meeting house is a two-and-one-half-story clapboard building with a gambrel roof, with the room for worship on the first floor. Collections include furniture, textiles, tools, farm implements, and folk art.

Continuing north, drive into the town of *Paris Hill,* off Route 26 above South Paris Village, along a street lined with old white houses with lovely gardens. These houses are open during a house tour sponsored by Stephens Memorial Hospital once a year. The *Birthplace of Hannibal Hamlin,* who was vice-president under Abraham Lincoln, is located just beyond the Hamlin Memorial Library. The library was once the Old Stone Jail, dating from 1828. From Paris Hill look to the west for spectacular views of the White Mountains.

This area is a destination for rock hunters because there are several mines to visit. Call (207) 674–2341 for more information on visiting mines. Or you can see gems at *Perham's Store* (207–674–2340) on Route 26 in West Paris.

Head for 109 Main Street, South Paris to *Maurice Restaurant Français* (207–743–2532), which is located in an old farmhouse in South Paris. European cuisine includes shrimp scampi, veal flambe, and duck l'orange.

Bethel

Continue north to Bethel on Route 26 at the junction with Route 2. Built on the banks of the Androscoggin River, the town is set in the foothills of the White Mountains. Settled in 1774, it is one of the oldest towns in the region. Besides serving as a center for lumbering and farming, Bethel attracts visitors for fishing, boating, rockhounding in local mines, and skiing. For a meal out try the *Bethel Inn* (800–654–0125 or 207–824–2175), *L'Auberge* (207–824–2774), or *Sudbury Inn* (207–824–2174).

Sunday River Ski Resort (800–543–2SKI or 207–824–3000) is only 6 miles away. Its growth tells one of the most remarkable stories in the ski industry, and most of that is due to the vision and persistence of Leslie B. Otten. He first came to a quite modest resort with five lifts and twenty trails in the 1970s when it was under the same ownership as Killington in Vermont.

In 1980 he purchased Sunday River and began two decades of intensive development that now covers eight mountains and 654 acres of skiable terrain with a vertical drop of 2,340 feet. Eighteen lifts, four of them detachable quads, now serve 126 trails with 92 percent snowmaking coverage. Although development on the mountain has been the priority, base facilities have also been improved. They include luxury slopeside accommodations at the *Grand Summit Resort Hotel* and the *Jordan Grand Resort Hotel and Conference Center,* which opened an eighteen-hole championship golf course during the summer of 1999 to complement other activities such as hiking and mountain biking. Sunday River is the flagship resort of eleven owned by the American Skiing Company.

Cross-country skiing is available at several locations, including *Sunday River Inn* (207–824–2410), *Bethel Inn* (800–654–0125, or 207–824–2175), *Telemark Inn & Llama Treks* at the base of Caribou Mountain (207–836–2703), and *Carter's Farm Market Ski Touring Center* on Route 26 in Oxford (207–539–4848).

Just beyond the Sunday River Bridge is the famed *"Artists Bridge,"* a covered bridge dating from 1870 that is popular with both painters and photographers.

Grafton Notch State Park is located 25 miles northwest on Route 26. Visitors enjoy views of Old Speck Mountain to the west, Baldplate Mountain to the east, Moose Cave, Screw Auger Falls with its 25-foot-deep holes worn into the rock of the riverbed, and Mother Walker Falls. The Appalachian Trail passes through the park and continues for 277 miles to the top of Mount Katahdin.

Rangeley Lakes

From Bethel continue north on Route 26 to Errol (just over the New Hampshire border) and take Route 16 northeast to the Rangeley Lakes region. Or for an especially scenic drive, take Route 2 east to Rumford and Route 17 north to the Rangeley Lakes. If you go through Rumford, a papermill town, look for *Penacook Falls* in the middle of town. Route 17 follows along the Swift River, which is popular with gold panners. Views of lakes and mountains unfold as you drive north along this road. The last part of Route 17 is the spectacular section opening up with a view of *Lake Mooselookmeguntic.*

The Rangeley chain of lakes includes Rangeley, Quimby Pond, Dodge Pond, Kennebago, Loon, Saddleback, Mooselookmeguntic, Cupsuptic, Upper and Lower Richardson, Aziscohos, and Umbagog. Streams connect the lakes to provide a wonderful network for boaters and fishermen.

Rangeley Lake State Park (South Shore Drive, 207–864–3858) offers swimming, fishing, boating, picnicking, and camping and serves as a base for hiking, which is very popular in this area. The *Appalachian Trail* crosses below the lakes just a few miles south of town.

East of the town of Rangeley, *Saddleback Mountain Ski Area* (207–864–5671) has a vertical drop of 1,830 feet. Saddleback, with an elevation of 4,116 feet, has the highest base elevation of any ski area in New England. Forty alpine trails served by two double chairs and three T-bars offer an uncrowded skiing experience locals call "elbowroom." Cross-country skiing is available from the Base Lodge on a 50-kilometer trail network.

Not far to the east of Rangeley, *Sugarloaf/USA* (Routes 16 and 27, Carrabasset Valley, 800–THELOAF or 207–237–2000) vies with Sunday River as the largest ski area in the state; anyone who has skied it knows that Sugarloaf is indeed a single big mountain with a vertical drop of

2,820 feet and 1,400 skiable acres spread out below the summit. Also a part of the American Skiing Company, it too has undergone extensive development during the past several years, both on the mountain and on the base below. Fifteen lifts, including four quads, serve 126 trails and glades with 92 percent snowmaking coverage. Its summit, at 4,237 feet, offers skiing above the treeline. Below, the **Grand Summit Hotel** is expanding, and there are new condominiums as well.

Because it is in the snowbelt, Sugarloaf slopes hold their cover through late spring. A friend once called it Maine's undiscovered secret, but that is no longer true as more skiers come to enjoy this remarkable mountain. We recall its ability to hold snow from a trip in May many years ago, when the base still held nearly seven feet. The area was scheduled to close the next week only because the local farmers tending the lifts had to plant their crops! *Nordic skiing* is also available (207–237–2000). Summer activities include golf, mountain biking, hiking, fishing, white-water rafting, and swimming. The public golf course is nationally famous for its spectacular scenery and challenging design.

Moosehead Lake

From Rangeley take Routes 4, 142, and 16 east to Solon, then Route 16 and scenic Route 201 to Jackman. Did you know that Benedict Arnold took this route along the Kennebec River on his tragic expedition to Quebec? Look for interpretive markers along the way. At Jackman turn onto Routes 6 and 15 to Moosehead Lake. As the largest lake in Maine, Moosehead offers a wealth of wilderness to explore. Visitors gather for white-water canoeing, hiking, moose watching, hunting, fishing, camping, ice fishing, cross-country skiing, and snowshoeing. Take the 34-mile *"Bow Trip"* on the Moose River for a wilderness canoe trip you won't forget.

Greenville, at the southern end of Moosehead Lake, is the home of the *Katahdin,* a 1914 lake steamship. Besides offering cruises on the lake, "Kate" also serves as the Moosehead Marine Museum (207–695–2716). There you can peruse exhibits on steamboats and logging.

Mount Kineo, which ascends from the lakeshore, was favored by Indians as a source of stone for tools and weapons. Try some of the hiking trails for spectacular views of the lake and area.

Northern Outdoors (800–765–7238 or 207–663–4466) offers an "Outdoor Adventure Resort" with mountain biking, horseback riding, fishing, and rafting. For a real adventure take a trip along one of the rivers in a raft. There are one-day trips on the Kennebec River, two-day overnight trips, and combination "pedal and paddle" trips available. The central reservation service for *Raft Maine,* an association of white-water outfitters, may be reached at (800) 723–8633.

Baxter State Park

From Greenville head south on Routes 6 and 15 to Abbot Village, where you join Route 16 heading east to Lagrange and Routes 155 and 6 to I–95. Head north to Exit 56 for Millinocket and take the road toward the entrance to Baxter State Park.

There, *Mount Katahdin,* at 5,267 feet, is one of the highest peaks in the eastern United States. The *Appalachian Trail,* which begins in Georgia, ends here.

In 1930 Perceval P. Baxter began purchasing the land around the mountain and later gave it "for the benefit of the people of Maine" to enjoy in its natural state. And enjoy it you will. You can swim, hike (be sure to check trail conditions with a park ranger), picnic, fish, canoe, and camp here. Contact Baxter State Park, Box 540, Millinocket, ME 04462 (207–723–5140), or stop at the park office at 64 Balsam Drive for maps, information, and a list of rules.

Canoeing enthusiasts dream about a lengthy trip along the *Allagash Wilderness Waterway,* a 95-mile stretch through lakes, rivers, and forests.

Chamberlain Thoroughfare, which lies between Lakes Chamberlain and Telos, is the best place to launch your canoe. The long paddle ends in Allagash Village, north of Allagash Falls. At this point the Allagash flows into the St. John River. You must register before beginning on this trip because rangers want to know where you are. Contact the Bureau of Parks and Recreation at (207) 287–3821, or write to Maine Department of Conservation, State House Station 22, Augusta, ME 04333.

Your taste of the lakes and mountains of Maine on this itinerary is complete. Continue to explore the vast backwoods regions of this state on your own or head back to the coast along I–95.

For More Information

Bethel Area Chamber of Commerce, 30 Cross Street, Town Train Station, P.O. Box 1247, Bethel, ME 04217; (800) 442–5826 or (207) 824–2282; www.bethelmaine.com

Greater Windham Chamber of Commerce, 835 Roosevelt Trail, P.O. Box 1015, Windham, ME 04062; (207) 892–8265; www.windham chamber.sebagolake.org

Jackman Chamber of Commerce, P.O. Box 368, Jackman, ME 04945; (207) 668–4820

Katahdin Area Chamber of Commerce, 1029 Central Street, Millinocket, ME 04462; (207) 723–4443; www.katahdinmaine.com

Moosehead Lake Region Chamber of Commerce, P.O. Box 581, Greenville, ME 04441; (207) 695–2702; www.mooseheadarea.com

Rangeley Lakes Region Chamber of Commerce, Lakeside Park, P.O. Box 317, Rangeley, ME 04970; (800) MT–LAKES or (207) 864–5364; www.rangeleymaine.com

Appendix

Inns and Bed & Breakfasts

The following list of inns, historic hotels, and bed-and-breakfast accommodations includes a selection ranging from those that are inexpensive to establishments worthy of a "big splurge" occasion. We have tried to include those with an interesting historical past and/or a beautiful setting.

On the whole, inns and B&Bs in the United States are more expensive than their counterparts in Europe, but they are more appealing than comparable motel accommodations. Some of them offer special rates during their off-peak times, such as weekends in cities and weekdays in the country, or at quiet times in their seasonal cycle through the year. Prices will vary, but all of them offer personal attention to make your stay pleasant; for once you will be something more than twenty to forty bytes on a computerized reservation list. Your host or hostess may offer you a glass of sherry, fresh fruit in your room, flowers, bath oil in the bathroom, or a foil-wrapped chocolate on your pillow. On the other hand, don't be disappointed by the lack of one of these gestures. You may find that your hosts will offer you an hour of conversation during an evening, and you may become friends and return year after year. Inn and B&B hosts and guests share one quality that appeals more and more to most Americans: They like to talk and to meet new friends in each region they visit, so it is no wonder that those who have traveled widely prefer staying in someone's home rather than in an anonymous hotel owned by a corporate chain. Almost all of the inns and B&Bs serve a complimentary breakfast, but only the inns serve lunch and dinner. Occasionally we have listed accommodations that do not fit the criteria for inns or B&Bs but are nevertheless the most appealing in the area.

Condominiums are springing up everywhere in vacation areas. Many beach and ski areas offer "condo" living throughout the year, and during off-seasons the rates drop considerably. Retirees with homes in the South often rent an inexpensive ski-area condo in the cool mountains for the summer. But even in high seasons, for leaf watching in the fall or skiing during the winter, condos may provide substantial savings for families who can cook their own meals rather than paying much higher restaurant prices. The initial price of the condo, which seems much higher than a lodge or motel, may be a bargain in the long run.

In no case do we pretend or intend to be comprehensive. We recommend good places that we know something of without prejudice to equally good places that we are ignorant of, many of which we hope to discover in future travels. Our listings of accommodations are neither inclusive nor exclusive—but only an adjunct to the book's itineraries for the convenience of those who do not wish to spend much of their time finding a good place to sleep.

Accommodations by State

Maine

Bar Harbor

Balance Rock Inn, 21 Albert Meadow, Bar Harbor, ME 04609; (800) 753–0494 or (207) 288–9900; www.barharborvacations.com. Once a summer home on the water, this inn has a gigantic rock balancing on the rocks below the house.

Bar Harbor Inn, Newport Drive, Bar Harbor, ME 04609; (800) 248–3351 or (207) 288–3351; fax: (207) 288–5296; www.barharborinn.com. The inn is located right on the water on the other side of the park from the public landing, maintaining privacy and yet closeness to town.

The Bayview, 111 Eden Street, Bar Harbor, ME 04609; (800) 356–3585 or (207) 288–5861; fax: (207) 288–3173; www.barharbor.com/bayview. Built on the water in 1930, this former private estate contains paintings, antique furnishings, and art objects from all over the world. Winston Churchill stayed here, and his portrait hangs over the fireplace in one bedroom.

Hearthside Inn, 7 High Street, Bar Harbor, ME 04609; 207) 288–4533; www.hearthside.com. This three-story weathered-shingled house was built around 1900 for a local doctor.

The Inn at Canoe Point, Eden Street, Route 3, Bar Harbor, ME 04609; (207) 288–9511; fax: (207) 288–2870; www.innatcanoepoint.com. This 1889 Tudor-style inn is located right on the water; you can walk on the rocks, through the woods, or enjoy the view from the deck or from any of the guest rooms.

Ivy Manor Inn, 194 Main Street, Bar Harbor, ME 04609; (888) 670–1997 or (207) 288–2138; www.ivymanor.com. Each room is decorated with Victorian and French antique furnishings. This Tudor-style mansion is set back from the street.

The Ledgelawn Inn, 66 Mount Desert Street, Bar Harbor, ME 04609; (800) 274–5334 or (207) 288–4596; www.barharborvacations.com. The inn was originally built in 1904 as a summer cottage for John Brigham, a Boston shoe manufacturer.

Manor House Inn, 106 West Street, Bar Harbor, ME 04609; (800) 437–0088 or (207) 288–3759; fax: (207) 288–2974; acadia.net/manorhouse. This 1887 mansion, on the National Register of Historic Places, is decorated with antiques. Accommodations are also available in the Chauffeur's Cottage and two garden cottages.

Bath

The Inn at Bath, 969 Washington Street, Bath, ME 04530; (207) 443–4294; fax: (207) 443–4295; www.inntraveler.com/theinnatbath. Antiques, portraits, and period furnishings fill the common rooms. Guest rooms are individually decorated; The Fo'c's'le has a private entrance.

Belfast

The Alden House, 63 Church Street, Belfast, ME 04530; (877) 337–8151 or (207) 338–2151; fax: (207) 338–2151; www.thealdenhouse.com. Four fireplaces have beautiful marble mantels. Comfortable bedrooms feature feather beds.

Belfast Bay Meadows Inn, 90 Northport Avenue, Belfast, ME 04915; (800) 335–2370 or (207) 338–5715; www.baymeadows.com. Accommodations are available in the main house and the newly converted barn. Five acres extend down to the water.

Belhaven Inn, 14 John Street, Belfast, ME 04915; (207) 338–5435; www.belhaveninn.com. This 1861 Victorian home has been renovated and is now a popular place for families, who may book several adjoining rooms. There's a circular staircase and twin parlors.

Jeweled Turret Inn, 49 Pearl Street, Belfast, ME 04915; (800) 696–2304 or (207) 338–2304; www.bbonline.com/me/jeweledturret. You can't miss the jewel-like turret, which is decorated with stained- and leaded-glass panels. Antiques furnish the inn, and a rock collection features semi-precious stones from each state set into an unusual fireplace.

The Thomas Pitcher House, 5 Franklin Street, Belfast, ME 04915; (888) 338–6454 or (207) 338–6454; www.thomaspitcherhouse.com. Thomas Pitcher built his home in 1873; it was one of the first in town to have hot and cold running water. The living room has a marble fireplace, and antiques fill the house.

The White House, 1 Church Street, Belfast, ME 04915; (888) 290–1901 or (207) 338–1901; fax: (207) 338–5161; www.mainebb.com. A marble fireplace, oriental rugs, paintings, and chandeliers decorate this home. Some rooms have water views.

Bethel

Bethel Inn and Country Club, Bethel, ME 04217; (207) 824–2175 or (800) 654–0125; fax: (207) 824–2233; www.bethelinn.com. This inn dates back to 1913. Five Colonial guest buildings, a golf course, town-houses, and recreational facilities provide year-round pleasure for guests.

The Chapman Inn, On the Bethel Common, Bethel, ME 04217; (877) 359–1498 or (207) 824–2657; fax: (207) 824–7152; www.chapmaninn. com. Dating from 1865, the house was built by a sea captain. Over the years it has been a store, a tavern, and a boardinghouse.

L'Auberge Country Inn, Box 21, Bethel, ME 04217; (800) 760–2774 or (207) 824–2774; fax: (207) 824–0806; www.laubergecountryinn.com. L'Auberge is located in a garden at the edge of town. This inn offers comfortable rooms as well as a dormitory.

The Summit at Sunday River, Bethel, ME 04217; (800) 543–2754 or (207) 824–3500; fax: (207) 824–3993; www.sundayriver.com. White Cap Village is accessible from Tempest and Roadrunner Trails; Brookside is adjacent to White Cap Base Area.

Sunday River Inn, RFD 2, Box 1688, Bethel, ME 04217; (207) 824–2410; fax: (207) 824–3181; sundayriverinn.com. Down-home cooking is served family style to groups of all sizes. The Sunday River Cross-Country Ski Center is located at the inn.

Appendix

Boothbay Harbor

Harbour Towne Inn, 71 Townsend Avenue, Boothbay Harbor, ME 04538; (800) 722–4240 or (207) 633–4300; fax: same as phone; www. acadia.net/harbourtowneinn. Right on the water, this Victorian inn offers harbor views. Rooms range from housekeeping units to a penthouse suite.

Bridgton

Highland Lake Resort, RR 3, Box 17, Route 302, Bridgton, ME 04409; (800) 797–5301 or (207) 647–5407 or –5301; www.highlandlakeresort. com. The resort is located on the lake and offers housekeeping units.

The Noble House Bed & Breakfast, Highland Ridge Road, Box 180, Bridgton, ME 04009; (888) 237–4880 or (207) 647–3733; www.noble house.com. The Victorian manor house was built by a senator around the turn of the twentieth century.

Camden

Blue Harbor House, 67 Elm Street, Camden, ME 04843; (800) 248–3196 or (207) 236–3196; fax: (207) 236–6523; www.blueharborhouse. com. A restored 1810 New England Cape with rooms in the inn or suites in the carriage house.

Camden Harbour Inn, 83 Bayview Street, Camden, ME 04843; (800) 236–4266 or (207) 236–4200; www.camdenharbourinn.com. Designated a historic Camden landmark, this 1874 inn is located on a hill with views of the harbor and Penobscot Bay.

Edgecombe-Coles House, 64 High Street, Camden, ME 04843; (207) 236–2336; fax: (207) 236–6227; www.camdenbandb.com. This bed and breakfast, furnished with oriental rugs and antiques, is located on a hilltop overlooking Penobscot Bay. It also offers apartments by the week.

Hawthorne Inn, 9 High Street, Camden, ME 04843; (207) 236–8842; fax: (207) 236–6181; www.camdeninn.com. This Victorian inn has views of the harbor and gardens to wander in.

The Maine Stay Inn, 22 High Street, Camden, ME 04843; (207) 236–9636; fax: (207) 236–0621; www.mainestay.com. This bed and breakfast is located in a handsome Colonial right in the historic district.

Nathaniel Hosmer Inn, 4 Pleasant Street, Camden, ME 04843; (800) 423–4012; fax: (207) 236–3651; www.nathanielhosmerinn.com.The home was built in the 1800s by sea captains.

Norumbega, 61 High Street, Camden, ME 04843; (207) 236–4646; fax: (207) 236–0824; www.norumbega.com. Here is a castle that is worth taking a second look at, with its dramatic towers, turrets, and angles.

Whitehall Inn, High Street, Camden, ME 04843; (800) 789–6565 or (207) 236–3391. The inn is listed on the National Register of Historic Places. People love to rock on the front porch in the antique wooden rockers.

Cape Elizabeth

Inn by the Sea, 40 Bowery Beach Road, Cape Elizabeth, ME 04107; (800) 888–4287 or (207) 799–3134; www.innbythesea.com. Condo-style units include a kitchen, patio or porch, and views of Crescent Beach.

Carrabasset Valley

Grand Summitt Hotel, Carrabassett Valley, ME 04947; (800) 527–9879 or (207) 237–2222; fax: (207) 237–2874; www.sugarloaf.com. Located at the Sugarloaf Center right on the slopes, the hotel contains a dining room and offers both rooms and suites with wet bar and microwave.

Sugarloaf/USA, Carrabasset Valley, ME 04947; (800) THE–LOAF; fax: (207) 237–3052; www.sugarloaf.com. Sugarloaf Inn is right on the slopes, offering full services. Condos are also right on the mountain, complete with fireplaces or woodstoves.

Cornish

The Cornish Inn, Route 25, Box 266, Cornish, ME 04020; (800) 352–7235 or (207) 625–8501; fax: (207) 625–3084. This restored, old-fashioned, village inn is located in the Lakes Region of Maine. Guest rooms are decorated with antiques and stenciled walls.

Deer Isle

Goose Cove Lodge, Box 40, Sunset, Deer Isle ME 04683; (800) 728–1963 or (207) 348–2508; fax: (207) 348–2624; www.goosecovelodge.com. Cottages and suites contain woodburning fireplaces and decks.

Pilgrim's Inn, Box 69, Deer Isle, ME 04627; (207) 348–6615; fax: (207) 348–7769; www.pilgrimsinn.com. This 1793 inn offers antique furnishings and water views.

Durham

The Bagley House, 1290 Royalsborough Road, Durham, ME 04222; (800) 765–1772 or (207) 865–6566; www.bagleyhouse.com. The kitchen of this 1772 house has a large cauldron once used to make candles and soap. Rooms include cozy quilts.

Eliot

High Meadows Bed & Breakfast, Route 101, Eliot, ME 03903; (207) 439–0590. This lovely Colonial house was built on a hill in 1736 by a merchant shipbuilder and captain.

Freeport

Atlantic Seal Bed and Breakfast, 25 Main Street, South Freeport, ME 04078; (877) ATL–SEAL or (207) 865–6112; www.firsttravelerschoice. com. This 1850 Cape Cod home overlooks the harbor. Each room is named for a sailing vessel built during that period.

Brewster House Bed and Breakfast, 180 Main Street, Freeport, ME 04032; (800) 865–0822 or (207) 865–4121; www.brewsterhouse.com. Furnished with antiques, this Queen Anne home is located two blocks from L.L. Bean.

Harraseeket Inn, 162 Main Street, Freeport, ME 04032; (800) 342–6423 or (207) 865–9377; fax: (207) 865–1684; www.harraseeketinn. com. The inn consists of two period buildings from 1798 and 1850 plus a modern (1989) addition.

Nicholson Inn, 25 Main Street, Freeport, ME 04032; (800) 344–6404 or (207) 865–6404; fax: (207) 865–6907; www.nicholsoninn.com. This inn dates from 1925 and has always been in the same family.

White Cedar Inn Bed and Breakfast, 178 Main Street, Freeport, ME 04032; (800) 853–1269 or (207) 865–9099; www.members.aol.com/ bedandbrk/cedar. Arctic explorer Donald B. McMillan once owned this home. One new room has a private entrance and a spiral stairway inside.

Hallowell

Maple Hill Farm Bed & Breakfast Inn, RR 1, Box 1145, Outlet Road, Hallowell, ME 04347; (800) 622–2708 or (207) 622–2708; fax: (207) 622–0655; www.maplebb.com. The farm is located on sixty-two acres, with trails and a pond.

Isle au Haut

The Keeper's House, P.O. Box 26, Isle au Haut, ME 04645; (207) 367–2261; www.keepershouse.com. This is an inn in a lighthouse. Arrangements need to be made in advance for a forty-minute trip on the mailboat from Stonington.

Kennebunk

The Kennebunk Inn, 45 Main Street, Kennebunk, ME 04043; (800) 743–1799 or (207) 985–3351; fax: (207) 985–8865; www.kennebunkinn. com. Dating from 1799, the inn has been completely restored by the owners.

Kennebunkport

Captain Fairfield Inn, Pleasant and Green Streets, Kennebunkport, ME 04046; (800) 322–1928 or (207) 967–4454; fax: (207) 967–8537; www. inntraveler.com/captainfairfield. Favorite rooms include Joan's Garden Room with handpainted furniture, and the Library Suite.

Captain Jefferds Inn, 5 Pearl Street, Kennebunkport, ME 04046; (800) 839–6844 or (207) 967–2311; fax: (207) 967–0721; www.captainjeffer dsinn.com. This Federal-style mansion has guest rooms named after favorite locations such as Ireland, Italy, and Charleston.

The Captain Lord Mansion, Pleasant & Green Streets, Kennebunkport, ME 04046; (800) 522–3141 or (207) 967–3141; fax: (207) 967–3172; www.captainlord.com. Guest rooms are named for Maine sailing ships. *Brig Merchant, Schooner Champion,* and *Ship Regulator* are favorites.

The Captain's Hideaway, 12 South Street, Kennebunkport, ME 04046; (207) 967–5711; fax: (207) 967–3843; www.captainshideaway.com. The Captain's Room has a king four-poster bed and a gas fireplace. The Garden Room features lilac decor.

The Inn at Harbor Head, 41 Pier Road, Kennebunkport, ME 04046; (207) 967–5564; fax: (207) 967–1294; www.harborhead.com. Guest rooms are enhanced by painted tiles and walls by the innkeeper. The Harbor Suite has a *trompe l'oeil* mural.

The Maine Stay Inn, 34 Main Street, Kennebunkport, ME 04046; (800) 950–2117 or (207) 967–2117; fax: (207) 967–8757; www.mainestayinn. com. This 1860 house has a cupola on top and a wraparound porch. Cottages are also available with kitchens and fireplaces.

Old Fort Inn, Old Fort Avenue, Kennebunkport, ME 04046; (800) 828–3678 or (207) 967–5353; www.oldfortinn.com. Guest rooms are handsome with English-style furnishings including Queen Anne chairs. Victorian memorabilia decorates the walls.

The White Barn Inn, Beach Street, Kennebunkport, ME 04046; (207) 967–2321; fax: (207) 967–1100; www.whitebarninn.com. Some guest rooms offer whirlpools, four-poster beds, and fireplaces. There's also a cottage next to the pool.

1802 House, 15 Locke Street, Kennebunkport, ME 04046; (800) 932–5632 or (207) 967–5632; fax: (207) 967–0780; www.cybertours.com/1802house. Golfers will enjoy this house, located next to the fifteenth green of the Cape Arundel Golf Club.

Kingfield

The Herbert, Box 67, Kingfield, ME 04947; (800) THE–HERB or (207) 265–2000; fax: (207) 265–4594; www.mainmountaininn.com. This renovated 1917 Beaux Arts–style hotel has thirty-three antiques-filled rooms, most with Jacuzzis.

Naples

Augustus Bove House, Corner Routes 302 and 114, Naples, ME 04055; (207) 693–6365; fax: (207) 693–3833; www.naplesmaine.com. One of the first summer hotels in the area, now a bed and breakfast.The house is located across the street from the lake.

Newcastle

The Newcastle Inn, Newcastle, ME 04553; (800) 832–8669 or (207)

563–5685; fax: (207) 563–6877; www.newcastleinn.com. This inn, which has been operating since the 1920s, is located on the Damariscotta River.

North Windham

Sebago Lake Lodge, White's Bridge Road, North Windham, ME 04062; (207) 892–2698; fax: same as phone; www.sebagolakelodge.com. The lodge is located right on the lake.

Ogunquit

The Cliff House, Box 2274, Ogunquit, ME 03907; (207) 361–1000; fax: (207) 361–2122; www.cliffhousemaine.com. Dating from 1872, the rooms have balconies with an ocean view from Bald Head Cliff. It was built by the wife of a sea captain with wood milled in the family sawmill in Ogunquit.

Orland

Sign of the Amiable Pig, Route 175, Orland, ME 04472; (207) 469–2561; www.bedandbreakfast.com/usa/maine/orland. The inn has four working fireplaces with a bake oven in the keeping room.

Portland

Andrews Lodging B&B, 417 Auburn Street, Portland, ME 04102; (207) 797–9157; www.travelguides.com/home/andrews_lodging. A 250-year-old home with lovely perennial gardens.

The Danforth, 163 Danforth Street, Portland, ME 04102; (800) 991–6557 or (207) 879–8755; www.danforthmaine.com. A bed and breakfast in an 1823 Federal mansion with a widow's walk, near old Port.

Pomegranate Inn, 49 Neal Street, Portland, ME 04102; (800) 356–0408 or (207) 772–1006; www.pomegranateinn.com. A bed and breakfast with exceptional art collection, located in Portland's Western Promenade.

Rangeley

Country Club Inn, Box 680, Rangeley, ME 04970; (207) 864–3831; www.countryclubinnrangeley.com. The stone fireplace in the living room is handsome and is set off by pine paneling.

Rangeley Inn, Box 160, Main Street, Rangeley, ME 04970; (8⃠ 3687 or (207) 864–3341; fax: (207) 864–3634. This turn-of-the-ce⃠ inn is located on the eastern shore of the lake. The wood-beam pub is pa⃠ of the original 1877 building.

Rockport

Samoset Resort, Rockport, ME 04856; (800) 341–1650 or (207) 594–2511; fax: (207) 594–0722; www.samoset.com. Located on 230 oceanfront acres, the resort has a wraparound view of Penobscot Bay, which is beyond its golf course.

Rumford

The Madison, Route 2, Rumford, ME 04276; (800) 258–6234 or (207) 364–7973; fax: (207) 364–7973; www.madisoninn.com. The inn is located on the Androscoggin River. Seaplane rides are available.

Searsport

Brass Lantern Inn, 81 W. Main Street, Searsport, ME 04974; (800) 691–0150 or (207) 548–0150; fax: (207) 548–0304; brasslanternmaine.com. This Victorian dates from 1850, when it was home to a sea captain. The English owner has collected pieces from England as well as Ethiopia.

Watchtide, 190 West Main Street, Searsport, ME 04974; (800) 698–6575 or (207) 548–6575; www.watchtide.com. There are nice views of the ocean from the garden and back of this restored 1795 house. Pumpkin-pine floors and antiques make the house warm and cozy.

South Harpswell

Harpswell Inn, 108 Lookout Point, South Harpswell, ME 04079; (800) 843–5509 or (207) 833–5509; www.gwi.net/harpswel. This 1761 inn overlooks a harbor for lobster boats.

Waterford Village

Lake House, Routes 35 & 37, Waterford Village, ME 01088; (800) 223–4182 or (207) 583–4182; fax: (207) 583–6618; lakehousemaine.com. The inn was established as a hotel in the late 1700s; later it was a stop on a stagecoach run.

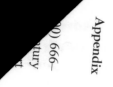
ite 1A, York Harbor, ME 03911; (800) 343–3869
x: (207) 363–3545; www.theyorkharborinn.com.
abin room," which is a real 1637 cabin that was
Isles of Shoals. Guest rooms offer Jacuzzis, four-
poster be ocean views.

New Hampshire

Bartlett

Grand Summit Hotel, Route 302, Bartlett, NH 03812; (888) 554–1900
or (603) 374–1900; fax: (603) 374–3040; www.attitash.com. This 1998
hotel is located right on ski trails belonging to Attitash Bear Peak.
Mountain views are everywhere. There's a health club with a steam room
and sauna and a heated outdoor pool accessed from inside.

Bethlehem

Adair, Old Littleton Road, Bethlehem, NH 03574; (888) 444–2600 or
(603) 444–2600; fax: 604–444–4823; www.adairinn.com. A hilltop mansion on 200 acres with the flavor of the early 1920s.

Bradford

Candlelite Inn B&B, Route 114, Bradford, NH 03221; (603) 938–
5571; fax: (603) 938–2564; www.virtualcities.com/nh/candleliteinn.htm.
This 1897 Victorian-style inn is located in the Lake Sunapee area.

Rosewood Country Inn, 67 Pleasant View Road, Bradford, NH 03221;
(800) 938–5273 or (603) 938–5253; www.bbonline.com.nh/rosewood.
The location of this inn is quiet, with beautiful woods all around. Each
guest room is individually decorated. Themes include Victorian,
Williamsburg, and Colonial styles.

Bretton Woods

The Mount Washington Hotel, Route 302, Bretton Woods, NH 03575;

(800) 258–0330 or (603) 278–1000; www.mtwashington.com. Dating from 1902, the hotel hosted the Bretton Woods Monetary Conference in 1944.

Colebrook

Rooms with a View, Forbes Road, Colebrook, NH 03576; (800) 499–5106 or (603) 237–5106; www.roomswithaviewbandb.com. This bed and breakfast is located on the side of a hill overlooking a valley. Guests can cross-country ski, snow-shoe, or snowmobile from the door in winter, hike or walk in summer.

Cornish

The Chase House, Chase Street, Route 12A, Cornish, NH 03745; (800) 401–9455 or (603) 675–5391; fax: (603) 675–5010; www.chasehouse. com. Rooms in the house date from 1766. The Gathering Room has hand-hewn posts and beams. Guest rooms are filled with antiques and quilts.

Dixville Notch

The Balsams, Dixville Notch, NH 03576; (800) 255–0600 or (603) 255–3400; fax: (603) 255–4221; www.thebalsams.com. Historic hotel on Lake Gloriette surrounded by mountains. It is popular for family reunions.

Exeter

Inn by the Bandstand, 4 Front Street, Exeter, NH 03833; (877) 239–3837 or (603) 772–6352; fax: (603) 778–0212; www.innbythebandstand. com. An 1809 inn with working fireplaces in every room.

Inn of Exeter, 90 Front Street, Exeter, New Hampshire 03833; (800) 782–8444 or (603) 772–5901; fax: (603) 778–8757; www.someplaces-different.com. This Georgian-style inn is on the campus of Phillips Exeter Academy.

Franconia

Franconia Inn, Easton Road, Franconia, NH 03580; (800) 473–5299 or (603) 823–5542; fax: (603) 823–8078; www.franconiainn.com. Located on 107 acres in Easton Valley with mountain views.

Lovett's Inn, Route 18, Franconia, NH 03580; (800) 356–3802 or (603) 823–7761; fax: (603) 823–8578; www.lovettsinn.com. A 1784 inn on the National Register of Historic Places.

Pinestead Farm Lodge, Route 116, Franconia, NH 03580; (603) 823–8121; www.pinesteadfarm.com. The views from this working farm include a meadow with cows, Cannon Mountain, and Kinsman Ridge.

Hampton Beach

The Grayhurst, 11 F Street, Hampton Beach, NH 03842; (603) 926–2584. This 1890 gambrel-roofed beach house has flower boxes totaling 30 feet in length.

Hancock

The Hancock Inn, 33 Main Street, Hancock, NH 03449; (800) 525– 1789 or (603) 525–3318; fax: (603) 525–9301; www.hancockinn.com. This inn has been operating since 1789, George Washington's first year as president. Guest rooms have four-poster or canopy beds, quilts and antiques.

Hanover

The Hanover Inn, Hanover, NH 03755; (800) 443–7024 or (603) 643–4300; fax: (603) 643–4433; www.hanoverinn.com. A nineteenth-century New England inn.

Hart's Location

The Notchland Inn, Route 302, Hart's Location, NH 03812; (800) 866–6131 or (603) 374–6131; fax: (603) 374–6168; www.notchland.com. The location is beautiful, with mountain views all around. The front parlor was designed by Gustav Stickley. There's a sun parlor blooming with plants. Each guest room is individually decorated; some have fireplaces.

Holderness

The Inn on Golden Pond, Route 3, Box 680, Holderness, NH 03245; (603) 968–7269; fax: (603) 968–9226; www.innongoldenpond.com. Dating from 1879, the inn property includes fifty-five acres, which are perfect for cross-country skiers. If you loved *On Golden Pond,* you'll love this inn's location. Squam Lake, where the movie was filmed, is across the road.

The Manor on Golden Pond, Box T, Route 3, Holderness, NH 03245; (800) 545–2141 or (603) 968–3348; manorongoldenpond.com. Built in 1903 by an Englishman, this inn maintains the charm of an English country estate.

Intervale

Wildflowers Guest House, North Main Street, Intervale, NH 03845; (603) 356–2224. This century-old country home has a lovely view of Mount Washington. The wildflower theme is carried out into the bedrooms; each has a different wildflower-patterned wallpaper.

Jackson

Christmas Farm Inn, Route 16B, Jackson, NH 03846; (800) HI–ELVES or (603) 383–4313; fax: (603) 383–6495; www.christmasfarminn.com. The original building dates from 1778, when it began life as a Cape Cod–style saltbox. More buildings were added, including a Baptist church, which was moved here on rollers. The inn is decorated for Christmas, and rooms are named after Santa's reindeer.

Eagle Mountain House, Carter Notch Road, Jackson, NH 03846; (800) 966–5779 or (603) 383–9111; fax: (603) 383–0854; www.eaglemountain.com. This is a historic hotel, dating from the turn of the twentieth century. Families meet here for reunions year after year. Cross-country ski trails pass right by the veranda.

Inn at Thorn Hill, Thorn Hill Road, Jackson, NH 03846; (800) 289–8990 or (603) 383–4242; fax: (603) 383–8062; www.innatthornhill.com. Views of the Presidential Mountain Range are savored from this 1895 Victorian inn. It is decorated with beautiful period pieces, including matching gentlemen's and ladies' chairs. Guest rooms are handsome, with carved headboards, marble-topped chests, and four-poster beds.

Nordic Village/Nestlenook Farm, Route 16, Jackson, NH 03846; (800) 472–5207 or (603) 383–9101; luxurymountaingetaways.com. Nordic Village, a family-oriented accommodation, offers condominiums. It has both indoor and outdoor pools, a steam room, and a therapy spa. Nestlenook Farm has seven guest rooms for adults. This historic B&B is on Dinsmore Road near the covered bridge.

The Wentworth, Route 16A, Jackson Village, NH 03846; (800) 637–0013 or (603) 383–9700; fax: (603) 383–4265; www.thewenworth.com. Views of the mountains are all around. There are a main building, five cottages, and eighty townhouses. The Thorncroft Suite is one to be savored.

Lincoln

The Mill at Loon Mountain, Lincoln, NH 03251; (800) 654–6183 or (603) 745–6261; fax: (603) 745–6896; www.mainstream.net/millatloon. The inn is part of the historic Mill at Loon Mountain, a newly renovated complex including the tavern in the former mill drying shed. Rivergreen condominiums and The Lodge Riverside Resort Hotel are also available through the same 800 number.

Lyme

Loch Lyme Lodge, Route 10, Lyme, NH 03768; (800) 423–2141 or (603) 795–2141; fax: same as phone. Lodge and housekeeping cottages.

Meredith

The Inn at Mill Falls, Mill Falls Marketplace, Route 3, Meredith, NH 03253; (800) 622–MILL or (603) 279–7006; fax: (603) 279–6797; www. millfalls-baypoint.com. In the early 1800s a gristmill and a sawmill were in full operation here, but they closed down before 1816. From the windows in the inn you can watch water cascade down through a series of channels. Accommodations are also available in the Chase House and Inn at Bay Point.

New London

Lake Sunapee Country Club, 100 Country Club Lane, New London, NH 03257; (603) 526–6040; fax: (603) 526–9622. The original building was designed by a golf course architect. It is popular with golfers in season and cross-country skiers in winter. The Norsk Ski Touring Center is here.

The New London Inn, 140 Main Street, New London, NH 03257; (800) 526–2791; www.newlondoninn.com. This 1792 inn is on the Town Green in the center of town. In winter there's a skating rink on one side.

North Conway

Farm by the River, 2555 West Side Road, North Conway, NH 03860; (888) 414–8353 or (603) 356–2694; fax: (603) 356–2694; www.farmbytheriver. com. This eighteenth-century home has been in the owner's family for seven generations. The B&B has sixty-five acres and fronts on the Saco River.

Nereledge Inn, River Road, North Conway, NH 03860; (603) 356–2831; fax: (603) 356–7085; www.nereledgeinn.com. This 1787 home includes a dining room and English-style pub where you can play darts, backgammon, and cribbage or just relax.

Portsmouth

The Inn at Strawberry Banke, 314 Court Street, Portsmouth, NH 03801; (800) 428–3933 or (603) 436–7242; www.users.rcn.com/sjglover. A nineteenth-century sea captain's house.

Sise Inn, 40 Court Street, Portsmouth, NH 03801; (800) 267–0525 or (603) 433–1200; fax: (603) 433–1200; www.someplacesdifferent.com. An 1880s inn decorated in the Queen Anne style.

Shelburne

Philbrook Farm Inn, 881 North Road, Shelburne, NH 03581; (603) 466–3831/3428. This 1834 home has been owned by five generations of Philbrooks. Antiques from the family adorn the guest rooms. The Presidential Range is visible from the inn, and the Appalachian Mountain Trail passes by.

Sugar Hill

Foxglove, Route 117, Sugar Hill, NH 03585; (888) 343–2220 or (603) 823–8840; fax: (603) 823–5755; www.foxgloveinn.com. A country home from the early 1900s in a woodland setting.

Sugar Hill Inn, Route 117 (Sugar Hill), Franconia, NH 03580; (800) 548–4748; fax: (603) 834–5621; www.sugarhillinn.com. The original beams, floors, and fireplaces grace this restored inn. A player piano stands in the pub.

Sunset Hill House, Sunset Hill Road, Sugar Hill, NH 03585; (800) 786–4455 or (603) 823–5522; fax: (603) 823–5738; www.sunsethill. com. An 1882 house set on a ridge with views of the Presidential Range.

Sunapee

The Inn at Sunapee, 125 Burkenhaven Hill Road, Sunapee, NH 03782; (800) 327–2466 or (603) 763–4444. The view from this 1875 house includes Lake Sunapee. The lounge has a fieldstone fireplace.

Waterville Valley

Black Bear Lodge, Waterville Valley, NH 03223; (800) 349–2327 or (603) 236–4501; fax: (603) 236–4114; www.black-bear-lodge.com. The lodge offers one-bedroom suites with a kitchen. Other amenities include an indoor-outdoor pool, whirlpool, sauna, steamroom, and gameroom.

Snowy Owl Inn, Waterville Valley, NH 03223; (800) 766–9969 or (609) 236–8383; fax: (603) 236–4890; www.snowyowlinn.com. The inn offers rooms, studios, and suites; a complimentary breakfast and wine and cheese or hot chocolate and cookies after 4:00 P.M. are included.

Woodstock

Woodstock Inn Bed & Breakfast, Box 118, Route 3, Main Street, North Woodstock, NH 03262; (800) 321–3985 or (603) 745–3951; fax: (603) 745–3701; www.woodstockinn-nh.com. Accommodations are in two houses. The Main House, a 100-year-old Victorian, is decorated with antiques. The Woodstock Inn Riverside overlooks the Pemigewasset River and has a porch for river-watching.

Vermont

Arlington

The Arlington Inn, Route 7A, Box 369, Arlington, VT 05250; (800) 443–9442 or (802) 375–6532; fax: (802) 375–6534; www.arlingtoninn. com. This Greek Revival mansion was built in 1848 by Martin Chester Deming, a railroad magnate and Vermont politician.

Barnard

The Maple Leaf Inn, Route 12, Barnard, VT 05031; (800) 51–MAPLE or (802) 234–5342; www.mapleleafinn.com. This Victorian-style farmhouse has a wraparound porch with a gazebo on the end. Guest rooms are pretty, with stenciling and quilts.

Twin Farms, P.O. Box 115, Barnard, VT 05031; (800) 894–6327 or (802) 234–9999; fax: (802) 234–9990; www.twinfarms.com. This property was once owned by Sinclair Lewis and Dorothy Thomspon, and some of the guest rooms are named for them. This gated, 300-acre estate is used as a retreat by those who want to get away and relax. Rooms are available in the main house and in cottages secluded in the woods. Favorites are Meadow Cottage and Perch.

Bennington

Four Chimneys Inn, 21 West Road, Route 9, Bennington, VT 05201; (800) 649–3503 or (802) 447–3500; www.fourchimneys.com. This historic inn offers French cuisine in elegant surroundings.

Burlington

Burlington Redstone B&B, 497 S. Willard Street, Burlington, VT 05401; (802) 862–0508; www.burlingtonredstone.com. This 1906 home is filled with antiques. The innkeeper delights in her lovely garden.

Willard Street Inn, 349 S. Willard Street, Burlington, VT 05401; (800) 577– 8712 or (802) 651–8710; fax: (802) 651–8714; willardstreetinn.com. The inn is furnished with antiques. Breakfast is served in the solarium.

Chester

Fullerton Inn, Box 589, Chester, VT 05143; (802) 875–2444; fax: (802) 875–6414; www.fullertoninn.com. A Vermont country inn located on the green.

Dorset

Barrows House, Dorset, VT 05251; (800) 639–1620 or (802) 867–4455; fax: (802) 867–0132; www.barrowshouse.com. This inn is almost 200 years old. There are a number of buildings on the property—some are perfect for a family or couples traveling together.

Cornucopia of Dorset, Route 30, Dorset, VT 05251; (800) 566–5751 or (802) 867–5751; fax: (802) 867–5753; www.cornucopiaofdorset.com. You can hear the chimes of the village church and walk to the Dorset Playhouse from this house. There's a cottage, Owls Head, behind the main building.

Dorset Inn, Church Street and Route 30, Dorset, VT 05251; (802) 867–5500; fax: (802) 867–5542; www.dorsetinn.com. The inn is located right on the Green, and early guests had a view of parades as well as the departure of the Green Mountain Boys in 1775.

The Inn at West View Farm, 2928 Route 30, Dorset, VT 05251; (800) 769–4903 or (802) 867–5715; fax: (802) 867–0468; www.innatwestview farm.com. Ten guest rooms are furnished with country antiques.

East Burke

Mountain View Creamery, Box 355, East Burke, VT 05832; (800) 572–4509 or (802) 626–9924; fax: (802) 626–9924; www.innmtnview. com. A historic country inn set on 440 acres.

East Middlebury

Waybury Inn, East Middlebury, VT 05740; (800) 348–1810 or (802) 388–4015; fax: (802) 388–1248; www.wayburyinn.com. Originally built as a stagecoach stop, the inn has been open for over 150 years. Guest rooms are individually decorated with four-poster canopied or brass beds. Meals include Sunday brunch.

Essex

The Inn at Essex, 70 Essex Way, Essex Junction, VT 05452; (800) 727–4295 or (802) 878–1100; www.someplacesdifferent.com. This country hotel includes restaurants operated by the New England Culinary Institute.

Goshen

Blueberry Hill, Goshen, VT 05733; (802) 247–6735; fax: (802) 247–3983; www.blueberryhillinn.com. The inn is located in the Green Mountain National Forest with pure air, no noise, and the chance to cross-country ski in winter or walk in summer.

Grafton

The Old Tavern at Grafton, Main Street, Grafton, VT 05146; (800) 843–1801 or (802) 843–2231; fax: (802) 843–2245; www.old-tavern. com. Chippendale and Windsor furniture make this an attractive inn. The building dates from 1801; it has been popular with writers over the years.

Jamaica

Three Mountain Inn, Jamaica, VT 05343; (800) 532–9399 or (802) 874–4140; fax: (802) 874–4745; www.threemountaininn.com. Dating from the 1780s, the inn has walls and floors of wide, planked pine, a fireplace, and a library for reading.

Jay

Jay Peak Ski Resort, Route 242, Jay, VT 05859; (800) 451–4449 or (802) 988–2611; fax: (802) 988–4049; www.jaypeakresort.com. Rooms are available in Hotel Jay; there are also slopeside condominiums.

Killington

Cortina Inn, Route 4, Box HCR-34, Killington, VT 05751; (800) 451–6108 or (802) 773–3331; in Canada (800) 635–7973; fax: (802) 775–6948; www.cortinainn.com. After a day on the slopes, skiers enjoy soaking in the inn's pool. The lobby contains a large open-hearth fireplace, and there is an art gallery upstairs.

The Inn of the Six Mountains, Killington Road, Killington, VT 05751; (800) 228–4676 or (802) 422–4302; www.sixmountains.com. A New Life Fitness program is offered in this elegant inn on the mountain.

Killington Grand Resort, 228 East Mountain Road, Killington, VT 05751; (877) 4–KTIMES; www.killington.com. This hotel is located right on the mountain. It offers a multitude of amenities.

Killington Village Condominiums, The Village Lodging Center, Killington, VT 05751; (800) 343–0762 or (802) 422–3101; fax: (802) 422–6788; www.killington.com. Six groupings of condominiums are clustered in the woods at the base of Killington.

The Summit, Mountain Road, Killington, VT 05751; (800) 635–6343 or (802) 422–3535; fax: (802) 422–3536; www.summitlodgevermont. com. Two Saint Bernards recline in the living room of this inn. Hand-hewn beams and four fireplaces add to the charm.

Landgrove

Meadowbrook Inn, Route 11, Landgrove, VT 05148; (800) 498–6445 or (802) 824–6444; fax: (802) 824–4335; www.meadowbrookinn.net. The Meadowbrook Ski Touring Center is right outside the door, offering 26 kilometers of marked and groomed trails.

Londonderry

The Frog's Leap Inn House, Route 100, Londonderry, VT 05148; (877) 376–4753 or (802) 824–3019; www.frogsleapinn.com. Dating from 1842, the house is surrounded by 200-year-old maples. Cross-country skiers can take off along the trails in the winter.

Lower Waterford

Rabbit Hill Inn, Route 18, Lower Waterford, VT 05848; (800) 76–BUNNY or (802) 748–5168; fax: (802) 758–8342; www.rabbithillinn. com. An expansion of an old tavern, this inn is located in a pretty village on the Connecticut River. Some of the guest rooms are called "fantasy chambers," and there are even secret doorways.

Ludlow

The Andrie Rose Inn, 13 Pleasant Street, Ludlow, VT 05149; (800) 223–4846 or (802) 228–4846; fax: (802) 228–3075; www.andrieroseinn. com. The living room has a handsome grandfather clock next to the fireplace. Some guest rooms have carved headboards and Laura Ashley fabrics.

Echo Lake Inn, Box 154, Ludlow, VT 05149; (800) 356–6844 or (802) 228–8602; fax: (802) 228–3075; www.echolakeinn.com. This inn includes rooms, suites, and new condominiums built in an old cheese factory.

The Governor's Inn, 86 Main Street, Ludlow, VT 05149; (800) GOVERNOR or (802) 228–8830; www.thegovernorsinn.com. The inn is located in an elegant Victorian home right on Main Street. Nine guest rooms are decorated with antiques.

The Okemo Inn, RD 1, Box 133-OM, Ludlow, VT 05149; (800) 328–8834 or (802) 228–8834; www.okemoinn.com. This inn is located 1 mile from Okemo Mountain.

Okemo Lodging Service, RFD 1, Box 165, Ludlow, VT 05149; (800) 786–5366 or (802) 228–5571; fax: (802) 228–2079; www.okemo.com. If you like to ski right from your door, this is the place. After a day of skiing or hiking, you can return to your condominium and build a fire in the fireplace. Each unit includes a complete kitchen.

Manchester Center

The Inn at Ormsby Hill, Route 7A, Manchester Center, VT 05255; (800) 670–2841 or (802) 362–1163; fax: (802) 362–5176; www.ormsbyhill. com. A 1760 home on the National Register of Historic Places; Ethan Allen hid in the secret room during the Revolutionary War.

Manchester Village

1811 House, Manchester Village, VT 05254; (800) 432–1811 or (802) 362–1811; fax: (802) 362–2443; www.1811house.com. This house once belonged to Abraham Lincoln's granddaughter. There is a pub where guests can play darts; they also can play chess in the library.

The Equinox, Manchester Village, VT 05254; (800) 362–4747 or (802) 362–4700; fax: (802) 362–4861; www.equinoxresort.com. The Equinox includes the Charles Orvis Inn and fly-fishing museum. The resort hosts the British School of Falconry, the Land Rover Driving School, a fitness spa, golf course, and myriad seasonal activities.

The Reluctant Panther Inn and Restaurant, Box 678, West Road, Manchester Village, VT 05254; (800) 822–2331 or (802) 362–2568; fax: (802) 362–2586; www.reluctantpanther.com. The inn is listed on the Register of Historic Places; it's painted purple.

The Village Country Inn, Route 7A, Box 408, Manchester Village, VT 05254; (800) 370–0300 or (802) 362–1792; www.villagecountryinn.com. An 1889 inn, once called The Worthy Inn, with rocking chairs on the porch and a magnificent Vermont stone fireplace.

Wilburton Inn, River Road, Manchester Village, VT 05254; (800) 648–4944 or (802) 362–2500; fax: (802) 362–1107; www.thisisvermont.com/

wilburton. A 1902 mansion built by Albert Gilbert, who was a friend and neighbor of Robert Todd Lincoln.

Middlebury

The Middlebury Inn, 14 Courthouse Square, Middlebury, VT 05753; (800) 842–4666 or (802) 388–4961; www.middleburyinn.com. This 1827 village inn has been restored; afternoon tea is served.

Montgomery

Alpine Haven, Route 242, Box 358, Montgomery Center, VT 05471; (802) 326–4567; fax: (802) 326–4009; www.jaypeakvermont.org. Chalets are equipped for housekeeping on a 700-acre estate. Condos are available at Alpine Meadows.

Black Lantern Inn, Route 118, Montgomery, VT 05470; (800) 255–8661 or (802) 326–4507; fax: (802) 326–4077; www.blacklantern.com. This restored country inn was featured in *Bon Appetit.*

The Inn on Trout River, Main Street, Montgomery Center, VT 05471; (800) 338–7049 or (802) 326–4391; fax: (802) 326–3194; www.troutinn.com. This 100-year-old Victorian country inn was built as a home for C. T. Hall. There's a trout stream and swimming hole on the grounds.

Mount Snow

Grand Summit Resort Hotel, Mountain Road, Mount Snow, VT 05356; (800) 664–6535; fax: (802) 464–4192; www.mountsnow.com. This full-service hotel is right on the slopes.

Mount Snow/Haystack Ski Area, Mount Snow, VT 05356; (800) 245–SNOW or (802) 464–8501; fax: (802) 464–4070; www.mountsnow.com. Condominiums, lodges, and country inns are available from these numbers.

Plymouth

Hawk Inn and Mountain Resort, Box 64, Route 100, Plymouth, VT 05056; (800) 685–HAWK, or (802) 672–3811, fax: (802) 672–5067; www.hawkresort.com. The resort offers tennis, swimming, and boating in summer and skating and ski trails in the winter.

Quechee

Quechee Inn at Marshland Farm, Clubhouse Road, Quechee, VT 05059; (800) 235–3133 or (802) 295–3133; fax: (802) 295–6587; www. pinnacle-ins.com/queecheeinn. This 1793 country inn has barn siding, rag rugs, and a large fireplace in the lounge. There's a cross-country ski center on the grounds. Summer activities include canoeing.

Shelburne

Heart of the Village Inn, 5347 Shelburne Road, Shelburne, VT 05482; 877-808–1834 or (802) 985–2800; www.heartofthevillage. com. This bed-and-breakfast is listed on the National Register of Historic Places. Attractive rooms are available in the main house or the carriage barn.

The Inn at Shelburne Farms, Shelburne, VT 05482; (802) 985–8498; fax: (802) 985–8123; www.shelburnefarms.org. An 1899 mansion on extensive grounds located on Lake Champlain.

Smugglers' Notch

Smugglers' Notch Resort, 4323 Route 108S, Smugglers' Notch, VT 05464; (800) 451–8752 (U.S.), or (800) 356–8679 (Canada), or (802) 644–8851; fax: (802) 644–1230; www.smuggs.com. The village includes condominiums, restaurants, pool, saunas, tennis, spa, skating, and skiing.

Stowe

Commodore's Inn, Route 100 South, Stowe, VT 05672; (800) 44–STOWE or (802) 253–7131; fax: (802) 253–2360; www.commodoresinn.com. Views from the Yacht Club Restaurant include model boats floating or racing on the lake behind the motel.

Edson Hill Manor, 1500 Edson Hill Road, Stowe, VT 05672; (800) 621–0284 or (802) 253–7371; fax: (802) 253–4036; www.stowevt.com. This country manor on 225 acres includes a cross-country ski center.

Fiddler's Green Inn, Route 108, Stowe, VT 05672; (800) 882–5346 or (802) 253–8124; www.fiddlersgreeninn.com. This homey Vermont farmhouse offers guests the chance to play chess or Scrabble in front of the fieldstone fireplace after a day of skiing.

Appendix

Stowe Resort, 5781 Mountain Road, Stowe, VT 05672; (800) 253–4SKI or (802) 253–3000; fax: (802) 253–2546; www.stowe.com. This resort offers slopeside accommodations in the hotel, townhouses, or condominiums; cross-country skiing on site.

Stoweflake, Mountain Road, Route 108, Stowe, VT 05672; (800) 253–2232 or (802) 253–7355; fax: (802) 253–4419; www.stoweflake.com. This all-season resort provides a swimming pool, health spa, tennis, golf, fishing, and skiing.

Stowehof Inn, Edson Hill Road, Box 1108, Stowe, VT 05672; (800) 932–7136 or (802) 253–9722; fax: (802) 253–7513; www.stowehofinn.com. This country inn has long views and Old World charm.

Ten Acres Lodge, Luce Hill Road, Stowe, VT 05672; (800) 327–7357 or (802) 253–7638; fax: (802) 253–4036; www.tenacreslodge.com. The 1840s lodge's living rooms have fireplaces and views out the bay windows over cross-country trails to the mountains.

Timberholm, Cottage Club Road, Stowe, VT 05672; (800) 753–7603 or (802) 253–7603; fax: (802) 253–8559; www.gostowe.com. The views from this home include the valley and the Worcester Mountain range.

Topnotch at Stowe, Mt. Mansfield Road, Stowe, VT 05672; (800) 451–8686 (from northeastern U.S.) or (802) 253–8585; fax: (802) 253–9263; www.topnotch-resort.com. This conference and resort center offers every activity a guest could want: tennis, swimming, horseback riding, games, racquetball, golf, billiards, lawn croquet, and a health spa.

Trapp Family Lodge, 700 Trapp Hill Road, Stowe, VT 05672; (800) 826–7000 or (802) 253–8511; www.trappfamily.com. This lodge offers a library, fireplace in the lounge, tennis, two pools, and a sports center. Austrian cuisine is featured.

Stratton Mountain

Stratton Mountain Inn and Village Lodge, Stratton Mountain, VT 05155; (800) 777–1700 or (802) 297–2500; fax: (802) 297–1778; www.strattonmountain.com. The inn offers 125 rooms or suites and a full range of hotel services. Also under the same management is the Stratton Village Lodge, located in Stratton Mountain Village.

Stratton Mountain Villas and Central Reservations, Stratton Mountain, VT 05155; (800) 843–6867 or (800) 787–2886, or in Vermont (802) 297–

2200; fax: (802) 297–4300; www.stratton.com. If you like to ski from your door, you can do it here. The villas have fireplaces for a warm glow after skiing, fully equipped kitchens, and washer and dryer.

Vergennes

Basin Harbor Club, Basin Harbor, Vergennes, VT 05491; (800) 622–4000 or (802) 475–2311; www.basinharbor.com. Dating from 1886, the property contains rooms in the main lodge, several houses, and cottages.

Waitsfield

Inn at the Round Barn Farm, RR 1, Box 247, Waitsfield, VT 05673; (802) 496–2276; fax: (802) 496–8832; www.theroundbarn.com. An unusual bed-and-breakfast with exposed beams, fireplaces, Jacuzzis, and an indoor pool.

Lareau Farm Country Inn, Route 100, Waitsfield, VT 05673; (800) 833–0766 or (802) 496–4949; www.lareaufarminn.com. Simeon Stoddard, the first physician in town, built this house in 1832; flatbread is baked on the premises.

Mad River Inn B&B, Tremblay Road, Waitsfield, VT 05673; (800) 832–8278 or (802) 496–7900; fax: (802) 496–5390; www.madriverinn. com. Built in 1860 and furnished with antiques.

Newton's 1824 House Inn, Waitsfield, VT 05673; (800) 426–3986 or (802) 496–7555; fax: (802) 496–4558; www.1824house.com. A restored farmhouse on fifty-two acres.

Tucker Hill Inn, Marble Hill Road, Waitsfield, VT 05673; (800) 543–7841 or (802) 496–3983; fax: (802) 496–3203; www.tuckerhill. com. An 1810 farmhouse with original beams and woodwork has been restored as an inn.

The Waitsfield Inn, Route 100, Waitsfield, VT 05673; (800) 758–3801 or (802) 496–3979; fax: (802) 496–3970; www.waitsfieldinn.com. Once a parsonage, the inn is furnished with antiques and quilts.

Warren

Beaver Pond Farm Inn, Golf Course Road, Warren, VT 05674; (802) 583–2861; fax: (802) 583–2860. A restored Vermont farmhouse with mountain views.

The Sugarbush Inn, RR1, Box 33, Warren, VT 05674; (800) 451–4320 or (802) 583–4600; fax: (802) 583–3209; www.sugarbush.com. A picturesque mountain setting offers rooms in the main lodge as well as townhouses. Cross-country ski network, ice skating, tennis, two pools, saunas, and whirlpool are on the premises.

The Sugartree Inn, Sugarbush Access Road, Warren, VT 05674; (800) 666–8907 or (802) 583–3211; fax: (802) 583–3203; www.sugartree. com. Canopy beds and lots of quilts as well as a sampler collection.

Waterbury

Thatcher Brook Inn, Route 100, Waterbury, VT 05676; (800) 292–5911 (U.S.), or (800) 336–5911 (Canada), or (802) 244–5911; fax: (802) 244–1294; www.thatcherbrook.com. This restored 1899 inn is decorated with Laura Ashley prints.

West Dover

The Inn at Sawmill Farm, Mount Snow Valley, Box 367, West Dover, VT 05356; (800) 493–1133 or (802) 464–8131, fax: (802) 464–1130; www.vermontdirect.com/sawmillfarm. Dating from 1770, the inn has an "old England" charm.

Weston

The Darling Family Inn, Route 100, Weston, VT 05161; (802) 824–3223. This restored 1830 farmhouse exhibits both European and American antiques.

The Inn at Weston, Weston, VT 05161; (800) 754–5804 or (802) 824–5804; www.innweston.com. This 1848 farmhouse is casual, yet elegant with its antiques. Cross-country skiers can take off from the door.

Windsor

Juniper Hill Inn, Juniper Hill Inn Road, Windsor, VT 05089; (800) 359–2541 or (802) 674–5273; www.juniperhillinn.com. This 1902 mansion is up on a hill with beautiful grounds and seclusion. The Great Hall is the place for afternoon refreshments. Guest rooms have antiques, and some have fireplaces.

Woodstock

The Charleston House, 21 Pleasant Street, Woodstock, VT 05091; (888) 457–3800 or (802) 457–3843; www.pbpub.com/woodstock/ charlestonhouse. This 1835 house is listed in the National Register of Historic Places. Some of the antiques inside belonged to the owner's grandparents.

The Jackson House Inn, 37 Old Route 4, Woodstock, VT 05091; (800) 448–1890 or (802) 457–2065; www.jacksonhouse.com. The original building was built by a sawmill owner in 1890. In 1996 an addition provided room for new suites and a restaurant. Each guest room is unique; a favorite is Francesca, with a cherry-wood sleigh bed, a fireplace, oriental antiques, and an Italian marble bathroom.

Kedron Valley Inn, Route 106, South Woodstock, VT 05071; (800) 836–1193 or (802) 457–1473; innformation.com/vt/kedron. This inn offers queen canopy beds, quilts, and fireside dining.

Village Inn of Woodstock, 41 Pleasant Street, Woodstock, VT 05091; (800) 722–4571 or (802) 457–1255; fax: (802) 457–3109; www.village innofwoodstock.com. This Victorian mansion offers homestyle New England dinners.

The Woodstock Inn, Woodstock, VT 05091; (800) 448–7900 or (802) 457–1100; fax: (802) 457–6669; www.woodstockinn.com. Built on the site of the original 1793 inn, this massive structure blends in well with this charming town.

Index

Index

About the Authors

Patricia and Robert Foulke have traveled together for forty-eight years, including four fellowship and sabbatical years in Europe, a three-month voyage in the Mediterranean, and numerous trips in the United States to research articles and update their guidebooks. Within the last twenty-three years, they have written books on New England, the Middle Atlantic states, and Europe. Their travel articles have appeared in the *Rotarian,* the *Christian Science Monitor,* the *Hartford Courant, Oceans Magazine, Greek Accent,* the *Detroit Free Press Magazine,* the *San Francisco Examiner,* the *Boston Herald, SAIL, Walking Magazine, Camping & Walking, Vista, USA, Sea History, Saab Soundings, Canoe and Kayak,* and *Senior Magazine.*

Robert completed his undergraduate work at Princeton University and received a Ph.D. from the University of Minnesota. He is a professor emeritus of English at Skidmore College in Saratoga Springs, New York. Patricia earned her master's degree at Trinity College in Hartford, Connecticut, and taught elementary school, remedial reading, special education, and writing classes until her retirement. The Foulkes live in Lake George, New York.